The Weyward Sisters

To Margaret, Deepak, and the memory of Lyta

The Weyward Sisters

Shakespeare and Feminist Politics

DYMPNA C. CALLAGHAN

LORRAINE HELMS

and JYOTSNA SINGH

BLACKWELL
Oxford UK & Cambridge USA

First published 1994

Blackwell Publishers
238 Main Street
Cambridge, Massachusetts 02142
USA

108 Cowley Road
Oxford OX4 1JF
UK

Library of Congress Cataloging-in-Publication Data
Callaghan, Dympna.
   The weyward sisters: Shakespeare and feminist politics / Dympna
   Callaghan, Lorraine Helms, and Jyotsna Singh.
      p.   cm.
   Includes bibliographical references and index.
   ISBN 0-631-17797-3. – ISBN 0-631-17798-1 (pbk)
   1. Shakespeare, William, 1564-1616 – Characters – Women.
   2. Shakespeare, William, 1564-1616 – Political and social views.
   3. Feminism and literature – England – History – 16th century.
   4. Women and literature – England – History – 16th century.
   5. Love in literature.   6. Sex in literature.
   I. Helms, Lorraine Rae.   II. Singh, Jyotsna.   III. Title.
PR2991.C34   1994
822.3′3 – dc20   93-40753
                                                            CIP

British Library Cataloguing in Publication Data
A CIP catalogue record for this book is available from the British Library.

Typeset in Garamond on 11/13pt by Best-set Typesetter Ltd, Hong Kong

All. The weyward Sifters, hand in hand,
Pofters of the Sea and Land,
Thus doe goe, about, about,
Thrice to thine, and thrice to mine,
And thrice againe, to make vp nine.
Peace, the Charme's wound vp.

Act I, scene iii, *The Tragedie of Macbeth,*
the First Folio (1623)

Contents

Acknowledgments   ix

Introduction   1

1 **The Interventions of History:** Narratives of Sexuality
  Jyotsna Singh   7

2 **The Ideology of Romantic Love:** The Case of *Romeo and Juliet*
  Dympna C. Callaghan   59

3 **Acts of Resistance:** The Feminist Player
  Lorraine Helms   102

Index   157

Acknowledgments

Collaboration, which can so enrich a project, can also, we have found, protract its completion. We are grateful to our editor, Simon Prosser, for his patient support throughout this process, and to Gerald MacLean for his encouragement.

We should also like to express our gratitude to Terry Eagleton, Jean Howard, and Phyllis Rackin, who read our manuscript for the press. Their generous responses encouraged us, while their astute criticisms have greatly improved the final version.

Parts of Lorraine Helms's chapter have previously appeared in *Theatre Journal*, vol. 41, no. 2 (May 1989), pp. 190–200, and in *New Theatre Quarterly*, vol. 8, no. 30 (May 1992), pp. 167–77. We are grateful to Johns Hopkins University Press and Cambridge University Press for permission to reprint this material.

Introduction

Our title takes its direct reference, of course, from the witches of *Macbeth*. For us *Macbeth*'s midnight hags are no longer the despised demons of critical and theatrical tradition. Instead, we derive from them the image of the Weyward Sisters, genial inhabitants of the imaginary space from which we launch this book. This is the space in which Lorraine Helms sets her hypothetical production of *Macbeth*. In this production, the Weyward Sisters appear as a troupe of clowns, acrobats, magicians, musicians, and puppeteers to present a very different kind of play within the play. Neither grotesque nor glamorous, the Weyward Sisters embody the theatricality of *Macbeth*'s witchcraft via the liminality of itinerant players. The way these players interpret the events of the plot may not at first be intelligible to those who are accustomed to seeing Shakespeare's play through the eyes of the title character. Yet, Helms argues, the Weyward Sisters work as closely with the Shakespearean text and draw more broadly on its theatrical traditions than contemporary interpretations of *Macbeth* as the tragedy of a soliloquizing soldier or the disintegration of a marriage.

The image of the Weyward Sisters, an ensemble of players who bring their various skills together to produce a play, is one around which our different feminist critiques appropriately constellate. We write collaboratively, believing that through collaboration we begin to redefine scholarship as a communal enterprise rather than as an isolated and apolitical act. Yet we do not thereby erase our individual identities: the newts and frogs we each bring to our cauldron come from distinctively different cultural positions and experiences. These positions and experiences configure our individual chapters, inflecting our voices with accents acquired in varied social and professional settings. We do not attempt to render these accents homogeneously, but let them stand here for the differences that must be mediated in any collective action.

Our contributions to this volume represent different dimensions of a feminist materialist approach to Shakespeare. In a climate where both materialism and feminism can be reduced to claims of political correctness, these terms require some explanation. In describing our work as feminist, we mean not merely that we discuss themes of femininity but that feminism informs our methods and purposes in writing literary and theatrical history. Gender, as Joan Wallach Scott argues, is "the knowledge that establishes meanings for bodily differences. These meanings vary across cultures, social groups, and time" (2). Recognizing this revises the writing of history as radically as the Weyward Sisters revise the staging of *Macbeth*: feminist inquiry produces not variations on humanist or historicist themes, but new and different knowledges of texts, traditions, and institutions.

In describing our work as materialist, we acknowledge the weight and pressure of material determinants over other dimensions of social life. But we also write in the shadow of what Heidi Hartmann has called "the unhappy marriage of Marxism and feminism." In the 1960s and 70s, feminists drawn to the agenda of the left recognized that Marxism's "sex-blind" investigations had erased gender as a factor in establishing and maintaining relations between labor and capital (Barrett, 1–13). The critical approaches they developed in response to this erasure comprise current materialist feminism, whose topics include the ideologies of gender as they operate within specific cultural contexts, the history of women's social conditions, the relations among feminist, socialist, and anti-racist politics, and the intersections of material and discursive practices in the cultural forms and social institutions of the past and present.

Focusing on these intersections, we hope to uncover areas of both continuity and change between "the Shakespearean moment" and our own postmodern condition. Material practices are stubbornly resilient, and a historicism that neglects continuity in order to celebrate change risks underestimating this resilience. For Catherine Belsey, "Materialist feminist history is supple, subtle, and complex: it has no place for a unitary and univocal metanarrative," for "all texts exceed their own unitary projects; all texts release new interpretations as we bring to bear on them different – and differential – reading practices" (264–5). This excess arises from the unstable and indeterminate nature of patriarchy itself (261). Like Belsey, we seek "new interpretations" that derive from "different – and differential – reading practices." At the same time, we want to affirm that even the most supple, subtle, and complex histories imply determinate political positions. Hence each of our chapters strives to register the intricacies of Shakespeare's representation of femininity without obscuring the unsubtle and all too stable oppression that constitutes the fundamental material condition of women in patriarchy.

Jyotsna Singh's chapter, "The Interventions of History: Narratives of Sexuality," argues that the sexual labor of the prostitute in early modern England is predicated on the repression of female desire. Singh writes "history from below," aiming to recover the history of women's sexuality from the sedimented layers of the past to create a record of those for whom there is little recorded history. Her account of female sexuality, unlike many historical accounts, does not attempt to recover the individual experience of women in the past, but to show how material conditions *assign* sexual subjectivity to the female prostitute, as they do to the wife. If specific subject positions (either "whore" or "wife") are assigned to women, does any possibility for resistance remain? Singh finds that resistances are irrecoverable at the level of the prostitute's experience, but not at the level of *reading* itself. Reading against the grain of the representation of prostitutes within Renaissance drama and contemporary cultural contexts, Jyotsna Singh's narrative implicitly entails a reconceptualization of history. Dramatic representations of prostitutes, drawing on Renaissance discourses of the seductive dangers of female sexuality, enabled and sustained the practice of prostitution. Thus the discursive sexualization of women, interarticulated with material practices geared to the fulfillment of male desire, can in part account for the degraded social status of prostitution and its corollary, the fact that prostitution is traditionally women's work.

Dympna Callaghan's chapter, "The Ideology of Romantic Love: The Case of *Romeo and Juliet*," develops an explicitly Marxist understanding of the new formations of sexual love that nascent capitalism required. In so doing, she extends and redefines psychoanalytic and new historicist readings of desire. Asking how *Romeo and Juliet* intersects with early modern changes in modes of production and with postmodern discourses of desire, Callaghan emphasizes the larger social mechanisms (such as the organization of production and the structures of family life) through which desire is produced, rather than the micro-historical phenomena engaged by psychoanalysis (the individual psyche) and new historicism (the anecdote). While most feminist discussions of romantic love have centered on the nineteenth and twentieth centuries, Callaghan opens the early modern period to this history of desire. She argues that the ideology of romantic love is among the most potent modalities of the real, material oppressions that women endure. Far from a benign discourse of love and marriage, this ideology excessively restricts the erotic, enforcing compulsory heterosexuality and naturalizing asymmetrical power relations between men and women. These constraints persist precisely because the ideology of romantic love is so persistantly seen as benign. "Feelings" of love are presented as evanescent and their enduring material effects occluded, as though romantic love were unmoored from all social conditions and constraints. The ideology of romantic love is, then, both a dominant discourse and a discourse of domination.

For Lorraine Helms, feminist history includes the present tense of performance. In her chapter, "Acts of Resistance: The Feminist Player," she investigates ways in which the material conditions of theatrical production affect the performance choices available to those who play the woman's part in contemporary performance. What choices are possible when playing Shakespearean roles that have traditionally incorporated the fears and desires of male directors, playgoers, actors, and even characters? Exploring what she calls "the politics of prosody," Helms evaluates the interpretive restrictions that the conditions of a masculinist stage enforce as well as those inscribed in the play texts. In Helms's search for strategies to restage Shakespearean play texts, the Weyward Sisters come to symbolize the achievement of a feminist practice that can be recovered from the play text and its theatrical traditions.

Our purpose, then, in each of the three essays is to engage afresh with the relation between Shakespare and materialist feminism. The political significance of this relation, however, demands further explanation. While feminist, Marxist, African-American, and gay perspectives have challenged the once undisputed interpretive privileges of the dominant culture, these multiple perspectives may, some would argue, serve only to diversify the commodity known as Shakespeare. Once enshrined, multiplicity may reproduce either the pluralist notion that Shakespeare can embrace an infinite variety of interpretations or its postmodern equivalent, the notion that an endless diversity of interpretations can subdue Shakespearean texts to the commodifying impulse of a market economy. For Fred Inglis, feminists and others are merely "crying their wares in the cultural marketplace" (58); for Edmund White, feminist criticism concentrates on "far-fetched reinter-pretations of the classics," ignoring "late-century ills–poverty, urban decay, violence . . . etc." (43).

It is of course evident that there is no causal relation between feminist work on Shakespeare and the resolution of, say, urban violence. We ac-knowledge distinctions between activism and both academic and artistic work, as we acknowledge those between criticism and performance, peda-gogy and scholarship. But our distinctions admit similarities as well as differences: to create brute oppositions can have unfortunate results. If arguments such as White's and Inglis's are taken to their logical conclu-sions, they sever both criticism and performance from political engage-ment. Ultimately, they deny artists and academics the right to exercise their skills in response to current political issues and events – exactly the consummation so devoutly wished by reactionary funding agencies during the recent "culture wars."

We therefore emphasize the political dimensions of critical and theatri-cal enterprises as they emerge in current practices of reading, writing, and staging. We articulate these current practices with such historical phe-nomena as the labor of prostitutes in Renaissance England, the material preconditions of modern romantic love, and the conventions of the Eliza-bethan stage, hoping thereby to suggest ways in which feminist work in cultural history can contribute to the politically significant enterprise of opening new conceptual space.

We also hope that such work can open physical spaces, and especially the classrooms and workshops in which Shakespeare is presented to stu-dents of literature and theatre. Recent political criticism has called for pedagogical strategies to disclose curricular practices that contribute to social subordination. Among these practices is the appropriation of Shakespeare for elite culture (Ferguson, 278–81). In response to (if not yet fulfillment of) these appeals for change, formalist literary criticism has given place to historicism and other theoretical approaches, while drama workshop leaders have created exercises and improvisations that bring the categories of race, class, and gender to bear on students' interpretations of Shakespearean roles (Shepherd, 88–107). Our essays, we hope, will be part of this ongoing change, contributing to classroom discussions and work-shop exercises. Callaghan's and Singh's chapters, for example, suggest ways in which the macro-political developments of economic production and social/legal sanctions have influenced the history of desire that continues to influence students' lives, while Helms's "politics of prosody" offers students a method through which playing Shakespearean verse can become a micro-political intervention.

In linking Shakespeare and politics, we do not intend to lose the pleasures of the play texts. The Weyward Sisters do not conjure adversarial politics from Shakespeare only to bemoan the dire consequences. They do however seek (and find) different pleasures than those the play texts offer to the dominant culture. If, in so doing, feminists seem to be "crying their wares in the cultural marketplace," recall that those "wares" are the stories we tell about the stories Shakespeare has told us. And if our stories seem at first "far-fetched," recall that feminist critics and players have indeed travelled great distances. We now invite all who will to join us.

Works Cited

Barrett, Michèle, *Women's Oppression Today: The Marxist–Feminist Encounter* (London, Verso, 1980).

Belsey, Catherine, "Afterword: a future for materialist feminist criticism?" in Valerie Wayne (ed.), *The Matter of Difference: Materialist Feminist Criticism of Shakespeare* (Ithaca, Cornell University Press, 1991), 257–70.

Ferguson, Margaret, "Afterword," in Jean E. Howard and Marion F. O'Conner (eds), *Shakespeare Reproduced: The Text in History and Ideology* (New York, Methuen, 1987), 273–83.

Hartmann, Heidi, "The unhappy marriage of Marxism and feminism: towards a more progressive union," in Lydia Sargent (ed.), *Women and Revolution* (Boston, South End Press, 1981), 1–41.

Inglis, Fred, "Recovering Shakespeare: innocence and materialism," in Lesley Aers and Nigel Wheale (eds), *Shakespeare in the Changing Curriculum* (New York, Routledge, 1991), 58–73.

Scott, Joan Wallach, *Gender and the Politics of History* (New York, Columbia University Press, 1988).

Shepherd, Simon, "Acting against bardom: some utopian thoughts on workshops," in Lesley Aers and Nigel Wheale (eds), *Shakespeare in the Changing Curriculum* (New York, Routledge, 1991), 88–107.

White, Edmund, "When the genders got confused: the Odd Woman, the New Woman, and the homosocial," *Times Literary Supplement*, April 12, 1991.

1

The Interventions of History

Narratives of Sexuality
Jyotsna Singh

Introduction

Making the silent spaces speak . . .[1]

In the past two decades, feminist engagements with Shakespeare's texts have opened up new perspectives on the culture and society of the Renaissance. Especially since the 1980s, as feminist scholars have moved away from liberalism – with its attendant myths of a unified subjectivity and an ahistorical universalism – they have consistently identified *history* as a crucial aspect of any cultural analysis. As a part of this process, feminist readings of Renaissance literature and society have drawn on new modes of historiography that correct the gaps and omissions of existing histories. Together with other marginal groups, feminists recognize the power of systems of representation, which authorize certain kinds of knowledge, while repressing and marginalizing alien discourses and modes of knowledge. Therefore, as Michel Foucault would argue, if women and others want to resist being cast as subordinate subjects within elitist histories, they must develop "alternative discourses" – or "antihistories" – that displace and disrupt the continuum presupposed by hegemonic historiographies.[2]

Joan Scott similarly draws attention to the power of signifying systems, and calls for a new historical investigation in which gender is used as a central analytic category, not only as it applies to kinship and familial ties, but also to education, the economy, (that is, the labour market), and the polity. Her method has some important implications for feminist historicist critics: it reveals the gender inflections of earlier, seemingly disinterested or "objective" modes of historical inquiry; it focuses on gender as a primary way of signifying relationships of power; and it seeks to disrupt the ideologies that lead to the "appearance of timeless permanence in binary gender representation" ("Gender," 94). Scott questions traditional Marxists for whom gender is simply a "by-product of changing economic structures" (88), and instead draws on Derrida's critical practice to argue for a historical "deconstruction of the terms of sexual difference" (92). Based on these assumptions, she develops a methodology for analyzing, among other things, the production of female subjectivity: in history, in ideology, and in language.[3]

As theorists of history, both Foucault and Scott emphasize the ways in which discursive modes shape and produce social practices, reminding us of the constructed nature of history. What are the implications of such findings for a feminist historiography? They make the task of feminist historians/critics particularly complex in that they have to tread a fine line between using and manipulating systems of representation and facing doubts about notions such as truth, meaning, and knowledge, based on naïvely representational notions of language. Of course, contemporary feminist history cannot escape its own discursivity; its goal, however, should be to disrupt the existing array of historical narratives through which social identities are formed so as to articulate new subjects within alternative social and political alliances.[4] Thus, by emphasizing both contradiction and discontinuity within existing social and sexual hierarchies, it can show how all roles are *assigned* and changeable rather than natural and inevitable.

Numerous studies examining the Renaissance patriarchy have charted two contradictory historical trends that coexist in an uneasy relationship with each other: on the one hand, they have reconstructed a rigidly hierarchical model of gender relations as naturalized in a variety of orthodox discourses, such as Church sermons, marriage homilies, anti-feminist tracts, and conduct books. On the other hand, they also suggest that such images of a static patriarchal order are often a mode of wishful thinking, given the later, contradictory accounts of social historians and demographers who testify to a perception of a "crisis of order" in the face of sweeping economic displacements.[5] A crucial signifier of this "crisis of order" is the recurring image of unruly, rebellious women – "women on top."[6] While this image is marginalized and denigrated in the "public transcripts" of a hierarchical society, it repeatedly emerges in dramatic practices, folk festivals, and other aspects of popular tradition. Faced with these contesting representations, can feminists pin down the experience of women's lives in terms of a pre-discursive "reality?"[7]

As a way out of this impasse, many feminist studies of the period attempt to make visible and to document the experience of women, often by searching for resistances *outside* the discursive constructions of the Renaissance patriarchy, as well as those of later male historians. Feminist anthologies of the 1980s, such as *Rewriting the Renaissance* and *Women in the Middle Ages and the Renaissance*, certainly "marked a significant step toward [providing] a fuller, deeper, and more nuanced view of Medieval and Renaissance women and the cultures in which they lived."[8] Yet materialist feminist critics have also been quick to recognize that gender categories produced both within and outside the dramatic and cultural texts are precarious and problematic. And as one critic definitively points out, "the relationship between women's experience and the construction of women in cultural representations is the most problematic area for feminist criticism."[9]

Facing these conditions, a feminist historiography must recognize both the potential and the limitations of its epistemology. It is no longer the central issue that such a historiography distances itself from the "master discourses" of normative history and its agents. Where it faces a more difficult challenge is in historicizing women's experience without recourse to essentializing strategies. As feminist historians have incorporated new and multiple stories or subjects into orthodox history, they have established, as Joan Scott suggests, that "histories are written from fundamentally different – indeed irreconcilable – perspectives or standpoints, none of which is complete or completely 'true'" ("The Evidence," 776). But simply foregrounding the experience of the formerly disenfranchised has a limited impact, unless, as Scott argues, we "attend to the historical processes that, through discourse, position subjects, and produce their experience. It is *not individuals who have experience, but subjects who are constituted through experience*" (779, my emphasis). Experience, in this definition, is not the seen or felt "evidence that grounds what is known . . . but rather that about which knowledge is produced" (780).[10]

Scott's critique of contemporary historians has useful implications for any interventionist, feminist historiography and criticism. It suggests the need for dislodging ideological categories such as black/white, heterosexual/homosexual, masculine/feminine or stereotypical roles of the worker, the black male, the third-world subject, among others. Such reading practices would "make visible the assignment of subject-positions" to different groups and individuals, thus illuminating mechanisms of subjection and resistance.[11] To elaborate, one can say that once we recognize that identities are multiple and shifting, marginal groups such as women, blacks, and others can experience a sense of self that initially may seem precarious, compared to the humanist illusion of coherence, but ultimately embodies a sense of agency transcending a naïve individualism. For instance, as women recognize the shaping power of contradictory cultural fantasies about them, ranging from sex goddesses to maternal icons, they may also learn how these images are mobilized to the service of oppressive material practices. Thus by dislodging existing categories of identity, feminist theorists also open the way for changing the *practices* that have been authorized by the given categories.

Such issues of essentialism and agency have figured prominently in the work of Shakespearean and Renaissance feminists as they have attempted to historicize the "experience" of women in the sixteenth and seventeenth centuries. Traditionally, as we know, critics interpreted gender relations, in both dramatic and cultural texts, in terms of supposedly universal themes about marriage, family, and heterosexual love. Today, by multiplying stories and subjects, Shakespearean feminists – from the 1970s to the present – have disrupted the transcendental paradigms of prior literary and social history. However, there is also an accompanying anxiety about retaining some sense of individual autonomy – an anxiety that raises legitimate questions for many feminists, to which Carol Neely offers one response:

> [she calls for] some area of femaleness that is part biological, part psychical, part experiential, part cultural and that is not utterly inscribed by and in thrall to patriarchal ideology and that makes possible female discourse, a women's literary history, a feminist critique which can do more than lament its own inevitable co-optation with oppression. ("Constructing the subject," 7)

Many feminists understandably resist or at least resent the "thrall" of social constructions. But they also recognize that a woman's multiple identity – "part biological, part psychical, part experiential, part cultural" – is inextricably caught up in a web of *social* and *material* determinations. In grappling in this way with the relation between experience and cultural representation, they may find it difficult to chart the dynamics of resistance among women in the Renaissance. How does one distinguish between the motivations of a scolding shrew like Kate who refused to assimilate within the family, or of a woman who became learned and literate, or of a woman like Alice Arden who murdered her husband? And if women like these broke away from the subservient roles naturalized by the patriarchal ideology of the time, were they doing so as an explicit rebellion or simply as a random response to material constraints and pressures?[12] As these questions foreground and hypothesize the motivations of individual women, they also push beyond the limits of the personal and toward a distanced, critical look at the systemic determinations of identity.

To illustrate these historical processes of identity-formation, I would like to focus on one marginalized group among women in the Renaissance: prostitutes. Most accounts of social historians tell us that prostitution was perceived as as a law and order problem and as a threat to the morals of men as well as to social institutions like marriage. Many vivid descriptions of the stews and bawdy-houses in and around London appear in narratives about the criminal underworld consisting of growing numbers of vagabonds, indigents, and petty crooks. And in part these accounts are based on the records of punitive institutions like Bridewell, revealing regular crackdowns on prostitution.

Frequently, in these records, the official attack on brothels is underpinned by an unease about potential disturbances in the social hierarchy and the ideology legitimating it. A society of brothels and prostitutes not only threatened the stability of the household and marriage, but also held the possibility of social unrest among the lowest classes, as manifested in their resistance to a strict work regimen.[13] According to Ian Archer: "[standard arguments] used to justify action against . . . unlicensed alehouses and brothels were the temptations they offered to gullible apprentices."[14] The story told by social historians, then and now, treats prostitutes as *one* demographic group in the criminal underworld, in part, perhaps because they seem to have left few personal accounts of their activities. What we mainly learn is that official institutions like the family, the Church, and the courts only acknowledged or accounted for the existence of prostitutes through repression or ostracism. And yet, considering that prostitution remained a flourishing business, one can also assume a complicity on the part of official authorities and male clients in allowing brothels to continue in the face of ostensible surveillance and restriction.[15] What is missing in most accounts of prostitution in the Renaissance, however, is the connection between the demonization of women's sexuality and the material practices geared to the fulfillment of male desire.

The terms, "harlot," "whore," "strumpet," and "courtesan" recur frequently in various Renaissance discourses: in consistory court records, sermons, moral treatises, and literary texts. Typically (and especially in sermons and moral treatises), these labels are mobilized to suggest that if women's sexuality is not contained within holy wedlock, it emerges as "whoredom." And accompanying such moral prescriptions is the persistent distinction between an "honeste and innocent wyfe" and a "harlot."[16] Clearly, it is the figure of the "whore" that keeps alive the spectre of an unrestrained female sexuality, representing women's "weak" and yet "dangerous" nature. Reading these typical accounts of the time, we can acquire a sharper image of how women in the Renaissance, especially prostitutes, may have experienced their social and sexual identities, even though the interiorized subjectivity of the individual prostitute remains inaccessible; more importantly, I believe, these narratives of desire show how the category of the whore is deployed in male fantasies in ways that elide the reality of prostitution as a social and economic institution.

It is not difficult to learn of the socio-economic changes that may have led growing numbers of women into prostitution in the early modern period. But while social historians testify to new modes of commodification – of women's bodies and women's labour – in the transition to early capitalism, many accounts of prostitution, then and now, use a moralizing rhetoric as an ideological cover for the "logic" of commodification. My purpose is to write a feminist history that does not promote prostitutes as either victims or heroes, but makes visible the processes by which they were cast off and denigrated by the Renaissance society. Extending this methodology to the study of Shakespeare's prostitutes in the final sections of this chapter, I examine the ways in which generic and social conventions come together in the creation of the prostitutes' roles in *1* and *2 Henry IV*, *Measure for Measure*, and *Othello*.

Wives and Whores in Renaissance England

> for your body
> Is like the common shore, that still receives
> All the town's filth. The sin of many men
> Is within you . . .
>
> Thomas Dekker, *The Honest Whore*

> Now will I question Cassio of Bianca,
> A huswife that by selling her desires
> Buys herself bread and clothes. It is a creature
> That dotes on Cassio, as 'tis the strumpet's plague
> To beguile many and be beguiled by one.
>> *Othello*, Act IV, scene i, 93–7

> Dwell I but in the
> suburbs
> Of your good pleasure? If it be no more,
> Portia is Brutus' harlot, not his wife.
>> *Julius Caesar*, Act II, scene i, 284–7

. . . there is no greater sin before the face of God than whoredom . . . for it bringeth everlasting damnation to all that live therein to the end without repentance, it also bringeth these inconveniences, with many more: videlicet, it dimmeth the sight, it impaireth the hearing, it infirmeth the sinews, it weakeneth the joints . . . and, in fine, bringeth death before nature urgeth it, malady enforceth it, or age require it.
>> Philip Stubbes, *The Anatomy of Abuses* (1583)

> In Whitecross Street and Golden Lane
> Do strapping lasses dwell,
> And so there do in every street
> 'Twixt that and Clerkenwell.
> At Cowcross and at Smithfield
> I have much pleasure found,
>> Seventeenth-century ballad

Taken collectively, these representations of prostitution signal an uneasy production of male subjectivity on the nexus of pleasure, desire, fear, and repugnance of female sexuality. Given the unhealthy conditions of most brothels in and around Renaissance London, many men must have feared sexual encounters with prostitutes, even while they continued to support the flourishing trade in female flesh. Of course, most people could make a connection between prostitution and the economic need of women, recognizing that, like Bianca, prostitutes and even courtesans have to "sell their desires . . . to buy bread and clothes." Yet many attacks on "whoredom," here and elsewhere, seldom consider the material needs of prostitutes, and instead, transfer the burden of moral iniquity onto the "immoral" women, while representing them as the repositories of "the sin of many men."

Related to this fear and repugnance of "immoral" women is the anxiety about wives turning into harlots – an anxiety that Portia ironically expresses when she complains of Brutus's neglect by evoking the image of the actual "suburbs," the site of the brothels. While Portia quite casually elides the word "harlot" as a misogynist slur on women and prostitution as a socio-economic practice, she reveals an anxiety about the fulfillment of male desire: is masculine sexual pleasure located in the individual body of the wife or in the anonymous, depersonalized bodies in the suburbs? Portia's ambivalence about the location of sexual pleasure – as well as about the validity of different locations – typifies some of the complexities of Renaissance discourses of female sexuality.

The denigration of prostitutes, for instance, is not unrelated to a fear of female sexuality and, specifically, of cuckoldry – a fear that emerges as a recurring concern in both social and literary texts and that is often a deter-mining feature of male identity. The origins of this fear can be found in popularly known precedents such as the views of the Latin Fathers of the early Church. It is generally noted that the Church Fathers such as Augustine and Jerome valorized celibacy over married fidelity. In their eyes, women were the descendents of Eve and responsible for the world's evils. Tertullian sums up their sentiments when he addresses women as follows: "Do you know that you are [each] an Eve? The sentence of God on this sex of yours lives in this age: the guilt must of necessity live too You are the devil's gateway."[17] Yet, it is precisely this attitude of demonizing women as the cause of men's sins that also led the Catholic Church surreptitiously to support the practice of prostitution, as Gamini Salgado tells us:

> When Henry II promulgated the Ordinance touching upon the government of the Stews in Southwark in 1161, a large part of Southwark had already been under the control of the Bishop of Winchester for over half a century. That an area which consisted mainly of brothels should have been episcopal property will surprise no one who knows about . . . the equivocal attitude of the Church towards the sin of lust and lechery . . . Lechery was certainly a sin, especially if clerics were guilty of it, but prostitution was another matter. "Suppress prostitution," wrote Augustine, "and capricious lusts will overthrow society". (49–51)

Of course, such open equivocations were uncommon, being effectively repressed by the official moral ideology. In fact, in most of the writings of Renaissance moralists, the frequent "description[s] of female vice" connect women's beauty with sin and hold them responsible for men's lechery and lust. To support their case, moralists often draw upon orthodox religious tradition as an endorsement of their views. As Ian MacLean suggests, "in the metaphorical and allegorical understanding of biblical texts, woman is often identified with sensuality" (16), and such associations became commonplace in diatribes against women.

A curious aspect of this preoccupation with female sexual power is evident in the pamphlet war regarding the controversy about women. While the attacks on women's "immorality" by pamphleteers like Joseph Swetnam paint a picture of all women as deceitful harlots, the so-called "defences" of women represent them as abstract embodiments of virtues such as chastity and piety.[18] Thus, in the pamphlets of "praise" the subject of female sexuality is obscured within a general appeal to all women to conform to static stereotypes of virtue such as those found in the Bible (Gosonhyll).[19]

Learning from these varied sources, we can easily recognize that formal conceptions of masculine desire in the Renaissance were inevitably dependent upon the notion of an idealized, but passive and sexually unthreatening, female beloved, clearly distinguished from a sexually dangerous whore. Ruth Kelso's important study of the ideal Renaissance woman identifies the burden placed on women by the courtly, often Platonic ideal of love − an ideal that naturalizes women as desirable abstractions of beauty and virtue. According to Kelso,

> Most [Renaissance] writers . . . carried on long arguments over whether perfection rests in loving or being loved . . . It is the lover who is active because he takes the initiative, makes the choice, pursues, wins, and holds the beloved. The beloved is passive, accepting, receiving . . . Thus to be loved is assumed to be a lesser thing than to love . . . The lover knows whether he loves and whom he loves and what sort of person he is loving and how he should treat her to love and hold. (152–3)

The fact that such conceptions of love and beauty obscure the obvious power dynamic of these relationships is not surprising, given that "most of the books on love are written for men, and almost all completely ignore the woman's part in what might be supposed to be necessarily a two-sided business" (137). And while male desire is clearly valorized, women's sexuality is barely acknowledged, except in purely passive terms.

Such moralizing conceptions fail to acknowledge that the sexual transactions between men and women – in and out of marriage – were mediated by the material aspects of their existence, and thus they perpetuate and even romanticize dependent roles for women. A revealing connection between the masculine control and definition of female virtue and men's economic power can be found in Erasmus's "A pithy Dialogue between a Harlot and a godly yong man: shewing how shee going about to catch him in her snares, was (by his forcible perswasions) caught her selfe, and converted to an honest woman." A part of a longer collection of dialogues by Erasmus, *Utile Dulce: Or Trueths Libertie* (1523, trans. 1606), this imaginary exchange between a young man, recently converted to virtue, and an experienced prostitute, paints a vivid picture of the life of a prostitute, though predominantly from the perspective of the male "rescuer." Sophronius clearly speaks from a lofty, moral pedestal, which at best is paternalistic, and at worst, self-righteously puritanical. Prior to his conversion, the young man, Lucretia informs us, was "woont to be the wantonnest of all wantons. No man did ever more often resort hither, or at more unseasonable houres than [he] hast done" (K 3). Now, she mocks him, "art thou come hither to preache? put on a hoode, get thee into a Pulpit, and there we will heare you, with your little beard." While the prostitute urges him "let us now live and be merry," she also reminds him that "Every man liveth by his trade, this is our trade, and this is our lands" (K 2).

The young man questions her about her livlihood, "You do all that you do for lucre, do you not?" Then he makes her an offer that reveals not only his generosity, but also his obvious means of providing practical assistance: "You shall loose no penny of that that you looke for, I will give you foure times so much, if you will but onely hearken unto me" (K 2). With sincere intentions, Sophronius offers to "help [her] to something towards [her] dowrie: or else leave this place . . . into the seruice of some honest matrone" (L). Erasmus's dialogue is happily resolved with the whore's conversion; "looke me out a seruice," she asks Sophronius, who leads her to live with an "honest matrone, where [she] shall be a while at [his] charge (L). What we have here is a magical transformation of her poverty through the benevolence of her former client, rather than any change in the economic conditions that drive and keep such women in the "trade."

Erasmus's desire to reform the whore is in keeping with a respected medieval tradition that stressed humane reform for whores, rather than punishment – a tradition going back the twelfth-century canonist Gratian, who allowed that a man could marry a whore to reform her.[20] However, from the writer's and his male subject's ostensibly benevolent perspective, female desire exists only in relation to masculine lust (whereby the whore is a "common sincke") or to men's concern for their moral and social identities ("I had rather renounce all . . . harlots, than to be disinherited of my [heavenly] father" (K 4)). And finally, the harsh materiality of a prostitute's life – her vulnerability to contagion from the "French pore" and to the violence of "drunken and mad whoremaisters" – is secondary to the threat posed by harlots, and by inference, by all women, to the virtue of men. A "good man of Rome," Sophronius tells Lucretia, warned him that ". . . though the lippes of the harlot drop as the honie combe, and her words be softer that Oyle, yet her feete go downe to death, and her steps take hold of hell, and her end will be more bitter than wormewood" (L). Thus, if prostitutes like Lucretia suffer social denigration and ill treatment unless they reform, it is not because this is an inevitable effect of their "unruly" female sexuality, but rather, because all women are discursively marked as potential sources of lust and sin and as dangers to male salvation.[21]

Such anxieties about women's potentially dangerous sexuality persistently recur in a variety of moralistic narratives of the period. While it is not possible to trace a full history of such attitudes in these pages, its boundary can be mapped on the rhetorical grid of other such discourses: Erasmus's fears of whoredom, for instance, find an echo in a later moral attack on "whoredom" found in Thomas Becon's well-known *An Homely against whordom* (1560). Becon's general diatribe against adultery sets him railing against "the outragious seas of adultery, whordome, fornication and unclennes . . . [that] overflowed, almost the whole world (Fl. clviii). He defines adultery as a sexual encounter between "a maried man with a woman beside his wife, or a wife, with any man beside her husband," and firmly restricts sexual activity to procreative purposes, prohibiting "al unlawfull use of those partes which be ordayned for generacion" (Fl. clviii). Overall, in Becon's clearly gendered discourse, his anxieties focus on the "whore" who threatens men's ethics and the institution of marriage as the foundation of social and moral order. Repeatedly, he chastises adulterers, as in the following cautionary tale: "to maintayne hys harlottes and whores, to continue in his fylthye, and unlawfull love: swelleth he not also with envy, agaynste others, fearing his pray should . . . be taken away from him" (Fl. clx). In this instance and others, Becon asserts a distinction between the *wife*, who draws his sympathy, and the *whore* who threatens "the most holye knotte and bonde of matrimony." He regrets that "through whoredome . . . the honeste and innocent wyfe [is] put away and an harlot received in her stede" (Fl. clxi), and wonders how men "for the love of an whore put away their true and lawful wives agaynste al law, right reason, and conscience?" (Fl. clxi). Central to Becon's concern for women, however, is an insistence on their sexual purity, as when he plaintively asks: "How many maids be deflowered, how many wyves corrupted, how many wydowes defyled, through whoredome?" (Fl. clx). To sum up, one can note that while Becon eschews all modes of "carnal" living and promotes "holye" wedlock, he consistently defines female sexuality in the context of male desire, whether it is contained in marriage or emerges in "whoredome."

It is clear that when moralists ranging from Erasmus's young man to Thomas Becon and pamphleteers like Stubbes and Swetnam cast a dire eye on women as "whores," their views buttress the calls to a repressive female purity and obedience that is the staple of marriage homilies, conduct books, and "defences" of women.[22] Of course, as in Becon, these prescriptions of female virtue are often clothed in a general attack on "whoredome" or sexual promiscuity practiced by both sexes. But the gender inflections of these diatribes mark women as "whores," unless of course, they can be made into "honest wyves." For instance, Philip Stubbes in *The Anatomie of Abuses* (1583), argues that "all men that have put away their honeste wyves be forced to take them again and abandon all whores or els taste of the Law." However, his anger against the objects of male desire is harsher: "let all whores be cut of with the sword of right judgment . . . there is no sinne in all the world, but these whores, and whoremaisters will willingly attempt, and acheive for the injoying of their whoredome" (F 12).

Such a disgust for "whoredom" (for which women provide the temptations) and the accompanying calls for female virtue are also found in popular ballads and jests. While randomly scanning the titles and subjects of numerous ballads – "The Joy of Virginity," and "The Lamentation of a Woman being Wrongfully defamed," for example – one repeatedly encounters such attitudes, often invoked in clichés and stereotypes. In these tales, women are called to preserve their reputations via sexual constraint. Helen of Troy, for instance, is evoked in one ballad to provide a simple cautionary tale, "The reward of whoredome by the fall of Helen":

> If I had used my gifts in vertues lore
> And modest livd . . .
> where now too late, I lothe my life lewd spent,
> And wish I had with vertue bin content.[23]

In most cases it appears that women's sexual experience is inscribed in terms of its absence and denial, the only allowance being given to procreative sex in marriage. Furthermore, even narratives of desire which are not univocal in their call for virtuous women do not escape the prevailing demonization of female sexuality. In Robert Greene's *The Conversion of an English Courtizen* (1592), for instance, a witty fantasy of feminine eroticism is contained within a conventional, set-piece tale about the conversion of a prostitute through the influence of a virtuous man whom she eventually marries. Following this young woman's decline, from her self-indulgent youth to prostitution, and subsequently to her conversion and marriage, we can clearly see how the moral "logic" of this cautionary tale is embodied in its structure. And, as Kathleen McLuskie astutely points out, even more telling is the way in which the narrative implies an inevitable connection between female sexual activity and prostitution, without considering or evaluating the role of men as consumers of sex.[24]

The young woman's early self-indulgences in themselves do not signal any certain potential for becoming a prostitute, if it were not for the moralizing digressions that direct our responses. The daughter of "honest and welthy parents," the young woman intially awakens to her beauty and sensuality not as a mode of wantonness, but simply as a youthful vanity:

> As my apparrel was costly, so I grew to be licencious, and to delight to be lookt on, so that I haunted and frequented all feasts and weddings, & other places of merry meetings, where, as I was gazed on of many, so I spared no glaunces . . . I went to see & be seene, and deckt my selfe in the highest degree of brauerie, holding it a glory when I was wayted on with many eyes. (240)

These early vanities, which lead to "a multitude of wooers" are arbitrarily yoked to an inevitable promiscuity by the digression of a "A watchword to wanton Maidens," delivered by the young woman's uncle. In this predictable advice he extolls a "Virgins honour" and defines the decorum for young women: "Neither Cozen, is it seemly for Maydes, to iet abroade, or to frequent too much company . . . For shee that is looked upon by many, cannot chuse but bee hardly spoken of by some . . . Maydens actions are narrowly measured" (243). Despite this advice, and without offering any reasons for her actions, other than her wilfull desire, the young woman moves beyond the "narrow measure" of social opinion to reject "a welthy Farmer . . . of some forty years" for a husband and choose instead, a frivolous young man as a "shifting companion" (246–7).

While Greene's narrative follows the young woman in bold pursuit of her own desires, it is quite telling, as McLuskie points out, that her several liaisons quickly transform her into an object of exchange between men, finally forcing her to shift for herself as a common prostitute ("Lawless," 107). In the brothel, she pays the heavy price exacted by society from women who claim their sexual autonomy. Here, in a bitterly ironic reversal of circumstances, the young woman's "freedom" to engage in sexual activity in effect drastically curtails her sense of agency as she is forced to "entertaine al companions . . . like a staule . . . refusing none that wold with his purse purchase [her] to be his . . . the oldest lecher was as welcome as the youngest lover" (268–9). Earlier in the narrative, the young woman feels empowered by being "wondred at by many mens eyes [and setting] their harts more and more on fire" (251); what she never comes to realize, however, is that she has power only as long as she can manipulate her role as an object and recipient of male desire. And whether she is a desirable maiden or a prostitute, her sexual allure can never escape the thrall of commodification in the society in which she lives. In the brothel she literally has the experience of trading her body, "pay[ing] a kind of tribute to the Bawde, according as the number and benefite of [her] companions . . ." (269), but Greene does not describe this transaction to reveal or criticize the commercialization of women's sexuality as a pervasive social practice; instead, he offers a forced "moral" resolution to the story, whereby the woman is converted through the young man's invocations of "God Almighty" and his future judgments of her sin.

Initially, Greene's narrative lures the readers into an imaginative space that offers a complex perspective on female sexuality: both as a source of pleasure and as an object of societal control. Finally, though, *The Conversion of an English Courtizen* conforms to the convention of a cautionary tale that demands the conversion of the fallen woman, followed by the "reward" of respectability through marriage. Thus, concluding with the marriage of the young woman with the man who rescues her both morally and financially, the narrative clearly inscribes her sexuality within the confines of marriage – for "performing the rights of marriage which is lawful and allowed before God" (274).

It is in the context of such repressions and denials of female sexuality that I attempt to historicize Renaissance prostitution – a flourishing, though much maligned, trade in female flesh. As a result, I hope to show the interconnection between the ideological constructions of female sexuality and the material conditions of women's lives – some aspects of which have as much relevance to an understanding of women's oppression today, as they did in the Renaissance.

Why should one isolate Renaissance prostitution as a way of understanding representations of women in literary and social texts of the period? How did the tangible conditions of prostitution bear upon the lives of women in general and on the institutions of marriage and family (within the heterosexual economy) in the sixteenth and seventeenth centuries? And how do Renaissance constructions of male desire endorse actual patriarchal power? To some, these questions may seem gratuituous. Many would argue, for instance, that prostitution is timeless and universal – "the world's oldest profession." A disturbing instance of this attitude was evident in a televised interview with the owner of a legalized brothel in Nevada a few years ago: the portly, middle-aged man quite pleasantly told viewers that while men would always need female prostitutes for the fulfillment of their desires, he was doing a service to the women by enabling them to function in comparatively safe conditions.

The brothel owner's self-justifications clearly valorize male desire as natural and inevitable, while obscuring the political aspects of such a representation. Even today, in our democratic culture, we cannot say that we have escaped stereotypical definitions of gender as women's desire, more often than men's, remains yoked to obligatory "virtue" even while, ironically, the female sexual body is valorized as a cultural icon and then transformed into a profitable commodity. The fact that such an imbalance in power/sexual relations between men and women has occurred and continues to occur does not imply that its manifestations remain similar – and that they are not worth inquiry. Instead, I think a feminist inquiry into categories such as "woman" and "whore" produced in the Renaissance can at least implicitly refer to the reality of the present, showing how lives and "experiences" of women are discursively shaped to endorse specific socio-economic systems.

Prostitution, Labour Conditions, and Social Displacements in Renaissance England

... a great nomber of dissolute, loose and insolent people harboured and maintained in such and like noysome and disorderly howses, as namely poor cottages and habitacions of beggars and people without trade, stables, ins, alehowses, tavernes, garden howses converted to dwellings, ordinaries, dicying howses, bowling allies and brothell howses. The most part of which pestering those parts of the citty with disorder and uncleannes are apt to either breed contagion and sicknes, or otherwise serve for the resort and refuge of masterles men and other idle and evill dispozed persons ...

From an injunction given to the justices of the peace in Middlesex
to suppress disorder, 1596 (cited in Kinney, 15)

The Kings most Excellent Maiestie, considering, howe by tolleracion of such dissolute and miserable persons, as putting awaie the feare of almightie God, and shame of the world, haue byne suffered to dwell besides London and elles where in Common open places, called the Stewes, and there without punishment or Correccion, exercise their abhominable and detestable synne, there hath of late encreased and growne such enormities, as ... engender such Corrupcion ... where ... the youth is provoked, inticed, and allowed to execute the fleshly lust ...

[To remedy this, the king] Comaundeth that all such Householders as under the name of Baudes [that have] kept the notable and marked houses ... all such as dwell upon the Banke, called the Stewes, neere London ... doe before the said feast of Easter cease and leaue of their victualling, and forbeare to retayne any Gest or strainger into their house ... [until] they have ... bound themselues ... in Recognizance not to suffer any such misorder in their house ...

Proclamation of Henry VIII against the Stewes, April 13, 1546
(cited in Aydelotte, 148–9)

Thou rascal beadle, hold thy bloody hand!
Why dost thou lash that whore? Strip thine own back;
Thou hotly lust'st to use her in that kind
For which thou whip'st her.

King Lear, Act III, scene vi, 160–3

The history of prostitution in Renaissance London reveals a pattern of unsuccessful suppression of the trade. In *A Survey of London* (1598), John Stow briefly touches upon a part of this history:

> ... in the year 1506, the 21st of Henry VII, the said stew houses in Southwarke were for a season inhibited, and the doors closed up, but it was not long ... ere the houses there were set open again, so many as were permitted for ... whereas before were eighteen houses, from thence were appointed to be used but twelve only. These allowed stew houses had signs on their fronts, towards the Thames ... as a Boar's Head, the Cross keys, the Gun, the Castle, the Crane, &c ... In the year ... 1546, the 37th of Henry VIII, this row of stews in Southwarke was put down by the king's commandment ... no more to be privileged and used as a common brothel but the inhabitants of the same to keep good and honest rule. (151)

Henry VIII's stern edict did not put an end to brothels after his death a year later, even though prostitution no longer had any official sanction in post-Reformation England. In 1550, the borough of Southwark became a part of London, a privilege for which the civic authorities had to pay Edward VI a thousand marks, and in this arrangement prostitution simply shifted its sphere of operation to the private and now wholly illicit sphere. In Elizabethan London, both the patronage and punishments of bawds and strumpets continued unabated (Griffiths, 43; Salgado, 52).

It seems the authorities decided that if brothels were to be allowed to continue, they must coexist with an apparatus of official regulation. Thus, in April 1553, King Edward VI gave to the city of London, his "house of Bridewell to be a workhouse for the poor and idle persons of the city" (Stow, 147). Bridewell became the prototype for national houses of correction, whose functions included a brief incarceration of petty offenders (among which were many prostitutes), but whose overall effect was a wider criminalization of the poor. An account based on Bridewell records gives a vivid picture of the functioning of this institution:

> The monarch granted the mayor and citizens or those appointed by them "power and aucthoetie to searche, enquyre and seke out" in suspected houses and locations in the city, the suburbs, liberties, and Middlesex, "all ydell ruffians and taverne haunter, vagabonds, beggars and all persons of yll name and fame". These miscreants were committed to Bridewell and examined, or punished and corrected "by any other waies or meanes ... as shall seem good" to the governors' "discretion" ... [Thus] the Bridewell bench

assumed wide-ranging powers to police immorality in the city, targeting those of "incontinent life" and taking steps to check the "increase of harlots". Idle, lusty "rogues and strompets" and "harlots" were carried to Bridewell. Indeed, the whore became a piece of "Bridewell baggage". The bench either issued warrants to apprehend bawds, pimps and prostitutes or constables, deputies and other officers acted upon their own initiative, perhaps guided to a particular 'bawdy' by report or 'fame'. (Griffiths, 42–3)

Facing correction at Bridewell also meant submitting to punitive actions such as whipping for whores, which was a very formal affair, conducted in the presence of the board of governors (Sharpe, 113; Salgado, 53). Surviving *official* accounts of contemporary, municipal regulations, fines, and records of punishments, such as those at Bridewell, have generally been the only means of reconstructing the "facts" about the lives of prostitutes. Paul Griffiths, in his study of the Bridewell records, states that they "tell us little about the social origin of prostitutes, how they viewed their work, and how long they had been in the trade . . . [Instead, these records focused on] the various contacts and links which gave London prostitution a measure of . . . permanence" (49). And Ruth Mazo Karras, in her feminist reading of prostitution in late medieval England, also sums up the limitations of the sources:

> The Southwark brothel regulations provide frustratingly little information on the prostitutes themselves and how the brothels and brothel keepers shaped their experiences. There is no evidence as to whether the prostitutes of the stews felt any group identity in contrast with illicit prostitutes or other women. While we may surmise that the choice of work as a prostitute was dictated by economic constraints, we do not know what made the prostitute choose to work in the stews of Southwark rather than illicitly elsewhere . . . The restrictions under which they operated left traces, but the prostitutes themselves have not, and one can only infer from their circumstances the choices they may have made. (426)

Thus we can only reconstruct their lives through textualized traces that record the experiences of these women. We do not hear the voices of these prostitutes that enable us to consider issues of individual and collective agency. In a cruelly ironic sense, then, we cannot find any "real" prostitutes who call for our empathy and understanding. We have enough evidence to imagine the exigencies of their existence, but never hear any complaints.

The "reality" of the prostitutes' lives from the late Middle Ages to the Renaissance can only be imagined by drawing on a network of narratives detailing economic and social changes in England. Few would disagree with Anne Haselkorn when she states that "one aspect of the whore's history remains a constant: throughout medieval and modern times, she has been looked upon with contempt" (2); however, the reasons for the prostitute's situation vary within different social formations at different periods. In seventeenth-century England, for instance, the increased growth of prostitution can be closely linked to two interrelated factors: the growing number of destitute and poor – vagrants and beggars, many of whom were women – and the effect of these economic displacements on women.

The historical picture before us is one which depicts the Elizabethan and Jacobean periods as a time of growing inequity or as the "century of the dispossesed."[25] Increasing and chronic destitution and poverty were characteristic features of the English economy in the early modern period – one sign of the tensions created by the gradual emergence of a market economy with its attendant social displacements (Amussen, 164–7; Kinney, 24–5). Observers of this period note that England suffered from a confluence of various strains on the economy, such as the enclosure movement and the changing agricultural economy, the sudden shift from home to foreign markets, the introduction of piece-work production in the home industries, population growth, inflation, and debased money" (Underdown, 20–33; Kinney, 19). One effect of these changes was a growing population of destitute and poor – vagrants, rogues, beggars, many of them women – a process that began early in the sixteenth century.

According to A. L. Beier, "fundamental to the problem in England was the changing relationship of the bulk of the population to the land . . . [among smallholders] those without land, apart from small crofts and gardens, rose from 11 percent in the mid-sixteenth century to 40 percent in the mid-seventeenth" (17–21). This dispossession resulted from a complex agrarian revolution that had different local manifestations, including enclosure practices for transforming agriculture from a communal to an individualistic pattern. This trend ended, among other benefits, rights for grazing on common lands and sometimes led to the extinction of large rural communities of small land-holders (Beier, 21–2). As this new social order emerged in the seventeenth century, it excluded the traditional smallholders, thus displacing thousands to the mercy of different kinds of wage-labor in London and day-labor in agriculture – a process vividly summed up by one historian: "the increasing numbers of the landless [were] driven from the ranks of the independent producer to those of the day-labourer, the cottager, the squatter on the waste, or the vagrant migrating [to the cities] in search of work" (Underdown, 28). Among these growing numbers of laborers, frequently wage-workers, many may have suffered in the face of erratic and shifting modes of employment and a decline in the purchasing power of money, and in fact found few channels of upward mobility.[26]

This breakdown and destitution of rural communities through enclosures is evidenced most vividly in petitions of the homeless and evicted men and women, among whom were many laborers, whose wooden shacks on the waste had been pulled down because of restrictive laws on unauthorized housing for the poor. For instance, in the early seventeenth century, many fines are entered in quarter sessions records "for building houses without the necessary quantity of land . . . [with petitions being made by laborers whom the law prevented from erecting] a cottage without four acres of land" (Clark, 74–6). A sampling of these petitions provides an eloquent, sad testimony to destitution: George Grinham of Norton-under-Hamblin in 1609 requests permission "in behalfe of himselfe, his poore wife and famelye . . . "for my building . . . of a little poore house for ye comfort of my selfe, my poore wife and children betwixt those other 2 poore houses on the glebe"; another petition from an Elizabeth Shepherd of Windley, in 1649, describes the particular plight of women, when she states that "she was in possession of a Certayne cottage situate in Chevin, which was pulled downe and taken away by the Inhabitants of Dooeffield, shee left without habitation and hath so Continued Twelve months at the least, shee being borne in Windley, and hath two small children" (quoted in Clark, 76–7). Her petition was initially blocked by a technical objection, namely that Elizabeth Shepherd was married and a woman's petition could only proceed from a spinster or a widow, but after another child was born, a joint petition was presented by "Ralph Shepherd and Eliz. his wife" and accepted by the court (Clark, 77).

Another woman, Mary Marchant, petitioning against a forcible eviction from her tenement, reflects the plight of many poor woman who were deserted, when she states that she lives in "good estimation" even though her "husbande being abroad and driven Away; and returning not backe Againe to her leaveinge [her] with a little girle" (quoted in Clark, 75).

Thus, in situations of destitution poor women were inevitably hard hit. For instance, if a small "husbandman lost his land, his wife often no longer could afford to keep a cow or use dairying as a means of subsistence . . . [and] these women of the lower strata may have been forced to sell their labour for wages, over which . . . they did not have the same control custom had given them over the acitivities . . . [of] housewifery" (Cahn, 38). In the face of declining domestic industries and the loss of small holdings of land, the family unit among the poor came under some strain. And these women were frequently thrown back on their own resources as, in some instances, the men took to the road in search for work and, in others, parishes forbade the settlement of laborers' families, as is suggested by an Anthony Addams's petition in 1618: "I most humbly crave your good aid," he pleads to the justices in the parish of Stockton, that "I may have a house there to bring my wife and child" lest they "perish out of doors" (quoted in Clark, 81).

Overall, poor women in the sixteenth and seventeenth centuries faced conditions of insecurity in a gradually developing wage economy that produced new and more stratified divisions of labor – both in agricultural and urban settings. Records of the period frequently note the low wages of women – for instance, in agricultural jobs, men that "pull peas have 8d. women 6d. a day"; or in Norfolk, the wages for a woman clipper of sheep were 6d. per day while a male clipper was paid 7d. (quoted in Clark, 62). Among the increasing numbers of destitute women forced to shift for themselves, and often their families, many were absorbed by the textile industries. This was not sudden or incidental, but a gradual process whereby "by about 1650, the trades in which women predominated [such as textiles] were characterized by low pay and low profit" (Cahn, 60).

Textile labor, especially spinning, frequently figured in schemes for reducing penury, idleness, and moral decline, especially among women and children. Orders for the workhouse at Westminster in 1560 read that "old Women or middle-Aged that might work . . . should be Hatchilers of the Flax; and one Matron over them. That common Hedges, and such-like lusty naughty Packs, should be set to spinning . . . Children that were above Six and not Twelve . . . should be sent to winde Quills to the Weavers" (quoted in Clark, 131). Wages for spinning were low, 1s. 8d. a week for a grown woman, who could easily become a pauper if this were her only means of support. Thus frequently, spinning was simply added to other forms of menial labor for women – a situation that continued well

into the seventeenth century as is evident from Thomas Firmin's concern
for the poor in 1678:

> . . . suppose a poor Woman that goes three dayes a Week to Wash or Scoure
> abroad . . . or a poor market woman, who attends three or four Mornings in
> a Week with her Basket, and all the rest of the time these folks have little
> or nothing to do; but by the means of this spinning are . . . kept within
> doors. (Quoted in Clark, 135)

Women workers received low wages, not only for spinning, but for
other aspects of textile production too. Those employed in silk manufac-
ture also frequently faced hardship: according to a pamphlet of the period,
calling for a protection of this trade, these women who were "Winders
and Doublers", were mostly "poor Seamen and Soldier's wives," possibly
deserted or widowed, who supposedly found a "comfortable Subsistence"
for themselves and their Families, and "[took] off a Burthen that now lies
upon several Parishes, which are at a great charge for their Support"
(quoted in Clark, 142). Earning no more than 1s. 6d. or 1s. 8d. a week,
their situation was typical of large numbers of poor women, forced to shift
for themselves in the face of a devaluation of their labor. And policies of
poorhouse administrators, according to Alice Clark and others, reflected
this devaluation of women's work such as spinning: they often gave poor
women spinning work, which paid low wages bound to keep the women
poor and to lead them into desperate work like prostitution in order to
survive.

It is in the context of such dramas of struggle and survival which took
place among the displaced and destitute women of early modern England
that one has to conjecture or imagine how and why so many women
entered prostitution. In these conditions,

> large numbers of poor people came to London, enlarging the slums and
> thereby creating fertile soil for the spread of prostitution . . . New recruits
> were obtained in various ways. If the wives or daughters of needy citizens
> could not be corrupted, the procuress could meet the carriers who brought
> young and innocent country girls to London looking for work. (Shugg,
> 295–6)

Some of these vagrant women coming to London were unmarried pregnant
girls, others were looking for truant husbands, and many were just pushed

into prostitution by the hope of improving their lot. In urban areas, these women were often cut adrift from their families, where prostitution "usually involved professionals . . . living in bawdy houses where clients visited them" (Beier, 53).

Studies of prostitution such as these show that frequently, women in the period faced a variety of pressures to sell their bodies, and the increase in the number of prostitutes was, at least in part, a result of unemployment, especially among the dispossessed rural poor. By the reign of Henry VIII, thousands of women driven to London for employment were forced to take to the streets in different situations: some were seduced by city "slickers," eventually finding their way to the growing number of brothels; others set themselves up as independent prostitutes or became mistresses. Thus, prostitutes were not a homogeneous group and were driven to the trade by different kinds and degrees of "necessity," though unemployment and population displacements were certainly overarching factors in the prosperity of the brothels.

In terms of the location of the stews of London, Southwark and Bankside were the most notorious – and the prototypes – of the time, though brothels could be found in other parts of the city as well as in a few other English towns. What drew crowds of potential clients across the Thames to the suburbs was a variety of attractions such as bear-baiting, cockpits, and daily performances in the theatres, thus institutionalizing prostitution in terms of other lucrative entertainment activities in Renaissance London. It is interesting to note that not only were brothels and playhouses geographically adjacent to one another, but were also discursively linked together as places selling their alluring but corrupt wares in a competitive marketplace. Stephen Gosson succinctly sums up this connection in his *The School of Abuse* (1579): "For they [the denizens of brothels] that lack customers all week . . . to celebrate the Sabbath flock to theatres, and there keep a general market of bawdry . . . every wanton and his paramour . . . every knave and quean, are there first acquainted" (quoted in Salgado, 58). The relation between theatres and whore-houses did not simply involve prostitutes and their clients, but also managers and owners. For instance, theatre owners, Alleyn, Longley, Henslowe, and others were brothel owners too, finding both enterprises equally profitable (Salgado, 58).

By the end of the sixteenth century, the number of brothels in the peripheral areas of the City had increased, and according to Burford,

"Hundreds of watermen operated all hours of the day and night (despite prohibitions) bringing men over the water from the City to the delights of the Bankside" (142). While prostitution was considered a moral issue in many debates of the period, the economic dynamics of demand and supply were occluded. All accounts testify to a fierce competition among brothels even as the issue of their legalization was always at stake. When Edward VI came to throne in 1547, his father's edict against brothels was still in effect, but it was obviously not rigidly enforced, as Bishop Latimer berates the young king in his sermon in 1549: "My lords, you have put down the Stews, but I pray you . . . you have but changed the place and not taken the whoredom away? . . . There is nowe in London [more] than ever was on the Bancke" (196).

In Queen Elizabeth's reign, prostitution was once again officially frowned upon, but according to Ian Archer, "With evidence of at least one hundred bawdy houses operating in the later 1570s, it is clear that the closure of the Bankside stews had a minimal effect on the availability of commercial sex in [London]" (215). Brothels also catered to a different classes of men, and were geared to the demands and means of the varied clientele. According to Burford and others, some Elizabethan and Jacobean brothels were quite luxurious and profitable. At the lower level, the women had to ensure the maximum number of customers in the working day. Some statistics show that in high-class brothels a woman might receive ten to twelve men a night and at the bottom, thirty was the average (171). Overall, the dynamic of demand and supply of sexual labor was complex, with varying links between "the prostitutes, the owners of the bawdy houses and their pimps [demonstrating] the level of co-operation among the brothel keepers who frequently pooled their prostitutes and maintained links with several pimps" (Archer, 213). If there was any kind of hierarchy of control, then it was the pimps and keepers who often controlled access in the brothels. According to Griffiths, Bridewell accounts suggest that the keeping of houses was a potentially lucrative business, but offer little information as to how the individual payments were negotiated, although the keeper obviously expected a share of each transaction (46–7). Another aspect of this dynamic was that "the more casual and mobile prostitutes [free of pimps], though nominally independent, were vulnerable to those from whom they rented accommodation, and lacked access to wealthier clients" (Archer, 213).

Venereal diseases were rife and a fact of life, though possibly less rampant in more luxurious settings. Bawds or Madams could either be like the Mistress Quicklys or Mistress Overdones of the time – somewhat bedraggled figures in the lowest haunts in Southwark or handsome, mature women running a successful business. But the system certainly produced many determined unscrupulous women who were not averse to using other women, once they found their own charms declining (Burford, 172). Thus, as feminist historians, we must resist idealizing those who probably suffered from varying degrees of social victimization. Our aim is not to prove the "virtue" of these women, who could often be unscrupulous and grasping, but to trace the path by which they arrived at prostitution as a mode of existence.

Poverty was a concern of many civic-minded people in Elizabethan and Jacobean England, like Stubbes and Latimer, for instance, but few viewed prostitution as an "aspect of poverty, and the prostitute as a victim" (Haselkorn, 15). The 1601 Poor Law enacted to relieve unemployment sent the idle to the house of correction. While the prostitutes were punished by whipping, according to Salgado, "there are many references in the literature of the time to beadles and watchmen being bribed to turn a blind eye to the brothels, one of the bribes being an offer of a free sampling" (53). Thus, ironically, Bridewell in certain instances could function as a brothel. The Bridewell depositions are a useful record of the crackdown on the more organized aspects of prostitution, but do not tell us much about the material conditions or social attitudes faced by women (Archer, 213). John Stow gives a contemporary perspective on the social ostracism faced by prostitutes:

> these single women were forbidden the rites of the Church, so long as they continued that sinful life, and were excluded from Christian burial if they were not reconciled before their death. And therefore there was a plot of ground called the Single Woman's churchyard, appointed for them far from the Church. (151)

The voices of moral authority did not easily forgive the prostitute for her sins, as is evident from William Harrison's rantings, which disclose some of the punishments suffered by prostitutes and others engaged in "whoredome":

> harlots and their mates by, ducking, and dooing open penance [dressed in white sheets in churches, in the marketplace] are often put to rebuke . . . I

would with adulterie and fornication have some sharper law. For what great smart is it to be turned out of an hot sheet into an cold, or after a little washing in the water to be let lose againe into their former trades? . . . As in theft therefore, so in adulterie and whoredome, I would be with the parties trespassant, to be made bond or slaves unto those that received their iniurie . . . or to be condemned to the gallies: for that punishment would prove more bitter to them than half an houres hanging, or than standing in a sheet, though the weather be neuer so cold. (225–6)

Anne Haselkorn's account of the punitive measures faced by prostitutes tells a different story to that of Harrison as she connects the treatment of these women to the larger social project of criminalizing poverty; in this context, prostitutes were an easy target, once they had been identified as "sinful." Thus Haselkorn argues, "the punishment for the prostitute – generally a whipping or incarceration in a house of correction – was not unlike the treatment meted out to a poverty stricken female if she had no family or means of support, or if she had been turned out by her family because she had been seduced" (16). Furthermore, given the prevailing social attitudes, a woman may prefer prostitution to the rigors of the house of correction. And as the world of stews had its own hierarchy, some also hoped to rise above their station to become a keeper of even a mistress or wife. Such an option "might appeal to an enterprising young woman far more than the idea of being an involuntary servant, with no prospect of escaping from this dreary treadmill" (Haselkorn, 16).

Prostitution was a way of making a living for many women facing material needs, but economics were hardly mentioned in the discourses of sexuality that regulated – or desired to regulate – human sexual behavior. In the Puritan emphasis on married love, for instance, the denouncements of prostitution were in accord with the Puritan ethic of thrift and hard work that produced the new middle classes. Yet, Puritan attitudes were rife with contradictions. For instance, Philip Stubbes in *The Anatomie of Abuses* (1583) calls for all those committing the "horryble fact of whoredom" to "be cauterized and seared with a hote yron on the cheeke, forehead, and some other parte of their bodye that might be seen (F 12)," and, like Harrison, feels that the existing punishments are too mild: "For what great thing is it, to stande two or three dayes in a white sheete before the congregation, and that somtymes not past an houre in a day, having their usual garments underneth . . ." (F 12). Countering this angry disgust of "whoredom" expressed in such tracts, were other Puritan attitudes that emphasized reform and redemption. Thus, frequently, reformers tried to give the sinners (prostitutes) work, or to get them husbands – the subject of many city comedies.[27]

Most accounts – then and now – make one fact clear: namely, that prostitutes were scapegoats, not only victims of economic inequality, but also of society's fear of women's potential sexual power. Francis Gouda, recently reviewing two contemporary books on nineteenth-century French prostitution, foregrounds an issue that is crucial to any understanding of the practice – the placing of "male desire at center stage" (13). The production of the role of the prostitute, Gouda argues, takes place within the "polymorphous configuration of male lust, patriarchal power, bourgeois fear, and the strategies of male fantasies" (13). The fulfillment of male desire took place within a similar configuration in Renaissance England as the patriarchal fantasy of women's sexual threat obscured the social displacements, poverty, and unemployment that led to the flourishing trade in female bodies. Here, I do not wish to deny women's desire and the power of sexuality – both male and female. But the question still remains as to whose desire takes "center stage?" All accounts of punishment, regulation, and the exigencies of prostitution do little to suggest alternative choices for women for expressing their desire and, more importantly, for escaping the discursive production of female sexuality as dangerous, yet vulnerable and marketable.

Shakespearean Prostitutes

1 *and* 2 Henry IV

When one considers some of Shakespeare's representations of prostitutes – Mistress Overdone, Mistress Quickly, Doll Tearsheet, and Bianca – it becomes obvious that Shakespeare was aware of the culture's anxieties about prostitutes as well as of the economic conditions underpinning these women's livelihood. Yet it is telling that in his plays prostitutes are minor figures, often the source of humor and derision. Names like Overdone and Quickly are meant to stir instant humor through sexual innuendo – producing nods and winks among audiences both within and outside the play. The prostitutes are typed in terms of their trade, figures of fun who often produce the comedy of the plebian subplot. Even the prostitute with the more ominous name of Tearsheet lightens the atmosphere in *2 Henry IV*.

Taking a purely formalist approach to the plays, focusing on genre and structure, one can relegate the prostitutes to the subplot in which they fulfill their generic function. I first study the prostitutes in the context of their generic functions – in the history plays, in comedies, and in the tragedies – and then examine the possibilities of reading against the dictates of the plot structure. The notion of "character," I believe, comes under pressure in the case of Mistress Overdone, Mistress Quickly, and Doll Tearsheet as their names foreground stereotypical identities, representations of the shared humor among men. On the Elizabethan stage, the humor was heightened, no doubt, by the boy actors who probably drew laughs by exaggerating the prostitutes' sexuality. In the case of the history plays, *1* and *2 Henry IV*, the significance of the prostitutes' role is determined by how we contextualize these texts within the larger cultural discourse about power, politics, and history.

According to Phyllis Rackin:

> [for] many new historicists [the history play] . . . was finally univocal, a discourse of the elite, shaped by the interests of the dominant classes, whose definitive speaker and auditor and ultimate source of authority was always the sovereign. Cultural materialists, on the other hand, have discovered a polyphonic discourse, where even the voices of the illiterate can never be fully silenced. They have emphasized the role of popular transgression and subversion, while new historicists have tended to construe subversion as already contained – and indeed often produced – by the dominant discourse. (42)

Thus much criticism of the history plays has debated whether they uphold the conservative ideology of kingship or explain history in terms of "force, fortune, and practical politics" (Rackin, 43).

These arguments offer a useful frame within which to chart the possibilities of resistance in these plays and foreground a crucial fact, namely that they serve as a site upon which an ideological struggle is waged: a struggle between what Rackin and others have described as the "logocentric, masculine historical record" and the dissonant voices of the lower classes and of women who are excluded by the official chronicles. Formalist criticism has considered these contestatory voices in terms of "various techniques of juxtaposition, inversion, and antithesis that enable us to watch the action from many points of view" (Baker, 844). In emphasizing this contrast in *aesthetic* rather than political terms, critics have treated the double vision of the history plays in benign, almost conflict-free terms. For instance, Baker tells us in his introduction to *1* and *2 Henry IV*:

> Shuttling from scenes of state and grave affairs to scenes of bawdy wit and dissipation, Shakespeare weaves a rich design where each detail is set against its contrasting and complementary opposite so that they may sharpen one another. (844)

While such formal analyses have their obvious uses, they overlook the plays' complex engagement with the historical tradition from which they are derived. The world of Eastcheap, placed outside the linear, chronological time of history, makes visible the provisional and constructed nature of the existing, patriarchal historiography. The tavern is clearly a theatrical world whose inhabitants experience their lives through constant improvisation. Again, Rackin explains this process: "The anachronistic paraphernalia of ordinary sixteenth-century life with which Shakespeare surrounds his lower-class characters bespeaks their affinity with the immediate theatrical occasion, their separation from the textualized world of the historical past" (234).

Such anachronistic juxtapositions of the elite and the commoners and of history and performance certainly disrupt the decorum of Renaissance historiography, produced in the "council chambers and battlefields" and recorded in "genealogies and chronicles."[28] And, as numerous critics have pointed out, every aspect of Falstaff's behavior and action makes him a threat to the history of kingship and royalty.[29] Furthermore, not only have critics noted how the raucous, make-believe world of the Boar's Head tavern interrupts and parodies the historical action, they have also read these interruptions in terms of class divisions. As Michael Bristol succinctly notes: "Falstaff is socially as well as ethically ambivalent. He is Sir John, but prefers to name himself Jack, the most versatile and familiar name for every nameless hero of plebian culture" (205).

Like Falstaff, the prostitutes are also considered a vital part of the "carnivalesque" plebian culture, and as a group their loudness and irreverence – and the laughter it generates in audiences – are seen as subversions of the official discourses of authority and power.[30] Describing Mistress

Quickly's role in this vein, Rackin expresses a view shared by others: "Shakespeare uses the illiterate, common woman to parody the discourse of written historical learning and to invoke the disorderly common life that transgresses the social and linguistic protocols dividing the name-able from the nameless" (245).[31] While it is obvious that the scenes at Eastcheap disrupt both the historical record and royal authority, there is a danger in *conflating* the representation of the prostitutes with Falstaff's role as a mediator between the two worlds. As a "Lord of Misrule" and the braggart soldier, Falstaff is also Hal's "father" who complicates our understanding of significant issues like lineage, masculine honor, and kingly authority. The prostitutes' relationship to the historical plot, however, is more ambivalent and distinct from that of Falstaff as well as that of other, elite female characters – such as Hotspur's wife – who represent more romanticized and domesticated embodiments of femininity.

Mistress Quickly and Doll Tearsheet are not "real" historical characters and neither do they in any direct sense alter the patriarchal myths buttress-ing the historical record of the English kings. Yet their satiric function in the play – as embodiments of an alternative, non-heroic mode of existence – does open up the space for a feminist reading which makes visible the class and gender roles assigned to them in Renaissance society. Whether Mistress Quickly good-humoredly acquiesces to Falstaff's outrageous demands or, in Part 2, Doll Tearsheet ferociously harangues Pistol, they constantly negotiate their identities within or against the class positions available to them, while also pointing to the connection between gender roles and class mobility.

In *1 Henry IV* (III. iii), in her first long exchange with Falstaff, Mistress Quickly repeatedly defers to Falstaff's social advantage, while constantly asserting her own respectablity. We clearly see how she has allowed Falstaff to manipulate her generosity: "I know you, Sir John, you owe me money, Sir John and now you pick a quarrel to beguile me of it. I bought you a dozen shirts to your back." Falstaff mocks at her livelihood, to which the other men join in, undoubtedly with nods and winks among the audiences: he complains: "This house is turn'd bawdy-house, they pick pockets" (III. iii. 98–9) and constantly denigrates her as a whore: "There's no more faith in thee than in a stew'd prune" (III. iii. 112); and both her vulnerability and her resistance to his mockery is apparent in the following exchange:

Falstaff: Setting thy womanhood aside, thou are a beast to say otherwise.
Hostess: Say what beast, thou knave, thou?
Falstaff: What beast? why, an otter?
Hostess: An otter, Sir John, why an otter?
Falstaff: Why? she's neither fish nor flesh, a man knows not where to have her.
Hostess: Thou art an unjust man in saying so. Thou or any other man knows
            where to have me, thou knave, thou!

(III. iii. 124–8)

Repeating Falstaff's phrase, the hostess is angry when she stumbles upon the unflattering *double entendre*, but nonetheless she unwittingly reveals a position that makes her seem sexually vulnerable. Mistress Quickly repeatedly denies Falstaff's attacks on her virtue, while stressing his knavery and her own respectablity, and yet she also defers to the latter's superior class position: "I am no thing to thank God on . . . I am an honest man's wife, and setting thy knighthood aside, thou art a knave to call me so" (III. iii. 118–21). Throughout Part 1, despite her playful and somewhat ambiguous sparring with Falstaff regarding her identity – as a bawd ("stewed prune") and as a "respectable wife" (Falstaff: "Go make ready breakfast; love thy husband, look to thy servants cherish thy guesse" [III. iii. 170–2] – a number of references point to the existence of Mistress Quickly's "husband" and later, in next play, she refers to herself as "a poor widow of Eastcheap" (II. i. 70).[32]

Overall, as Jean Howard suggests, "in Part I, the tavern world is connected with lawlessness . . . [but] no pronounced sense of sexual licentiousness hangs over the tavern. In Part II, Quickly seems to lose her husband at the same time she acquires Doll Tearsheet as her friend" (44). Thus, whatever her past condition, Mistress Quickly's immediate concern in Part 2 is to improve her social status, preferably through marriage, which explains her indulgence of Falstaff. Instead of living a life of ignorant "immorality," as the moralists of the time would have us believe, Mistress Quickly repeatedly demonstrates an acute class consciousness and a desire to become socially and morally acceptable. While a bawd's life may afford her a mode of subsistence, it blocks any hope of social improvement without a "respectable" marriage. Falstaff no doubt plays on her social aspirations, as is apparent in her complaint in *2 Henry IV*:

. . . thou didst swear to me then, as I was washing thy wound, to marry me, to make me my lady, thy wife. Canst thou deny it? Did not goodwife Keech, the butcher's wife, come in then, and call me gossip Quickly? . . . And didst thou not, when she was gone down stairs, desire me to be no more so familiarity with such poor people, saying that ere long they should call me madam? (II. i. 91–101)

The hostess of the Boars Head tavern is not only concerned with her social status, but also with the decorum and reputation of her house. She is troubled when "Master Dumbe," her minister, says: "Neighbor Quickly . . . receive those that are civil, for . . . you are in an ill name . . . For . . . you are an honest woman, and well thought on, therefore take heed what guests you receive. Receive . . . no swaggering companions" (II. iv. 89–94). Mistress Quickly's concerns and ambitions are clearly imbricated in prevailing standards of respectability, even though her trade makes such aspirations an obvious source of humor and mockery for many members of the audience. She recognizes her own vulnerability in being "fubb'd off" by a predator like Falstaff and resents that "a woman should be made an ass and a beast, to bear every knave's wrong" (II. i. 37–8). And in response, she appropriates the label of an "honest woman" and seeks recourse from the officers of the law. However, the demands of comedy quickly make a mockery of Mistress Quickly's determination to seek reparation from Falstaff and to become an "honest woman." Within the logic of comedy, and in most typical performances, audiences are amused by the travails of Mistress Quickly, laughing at the ironic gap between her desire to be a respectable woman and her socially precarious position as a bawd. Thus, we have to ask that if, in Bakhtininan terms, the laughter provoked by Mistress Quickly is coming "from below," who is being empowered in its parody? Of course, few would argue that Mistress Quickly's carnivalesque malapropisms mock at the linguistic order buttressing the world of kingly hierarchy. However, she is also a source of laughter, a butt of jokes that have little subversive impact because they leave the *categories of social representation* largely untouched. In the world of the tavern, Mistress Quickly has no way of becoming an "honest" woman though she does try to overcome the distinctions between bawd and wife.

Doll Tearsheet also provokes the laughter of the audiences in Part 2, but with more disturbing echoes. In her, Shakespeare completely demystifies romantic conceptions of pleasure, desire, and female sexuality. We first learn of her in the exchange between Prince Hal and Poins.

Prince: This Doll Tearsheet should be some road.
Poins: I warrant you, as common as the way between Saint Albons and London.
(II. ii. 166–8)

Later, Falstaff also stresses her "common" status and reminds us of the most negative aspect of prostitution, evoked by her name "Tearsheet": ". . . you help to make the diseases, Doll. We catch of you, Doll, we catch of you" (II. iv. 44–6). Unlike Mistress Quickly, Doll Tearsheet does not aspire to "better" herself through marriage and experiences herself as "a poor whore . . . in a bawdy-house;" "I am meat for your master (II. iv. 126)," she tells Pistol, but does not play her part submissively, drinking "too much canaries" and shouting at her clients abusively – "A pox damn you, you muddy rascal" (II. iv. 39). Social position does not entirely escape her notice either, and she prefers the master, Falstaff, to Pistol, "scurvy companion" (II. iv. 123). But her abusive language also reveals the brothel to be a sordid world where all the niceties of social and class distinctions are erased. If Doll perceives herself as "meat" in a place where pleasures of the flesh are bought and sold, then she views her clients as none other than "whoreson[s]" (II. iv. 218). Thus, not surprisingly, she casts a cynical eye on any pretentions of male honor and valor. Pistol's claims of military status meet with her derision: "Captain, thou abominable damn'd cheater, art thou not asham'd to be call'd captain? . . . You a captain! you slave, for what? for tearing a poor whore's ruff in a bawdy-house?" (II. iv. 140–5). Later, even her endearments toward Falstaff deflate his "valour:" she praises him for fighting Pistol ("thou art as valorous as Hector" (II. iv. 219), but soon reminds him of his mortality: "Thou whoreson little tidy Bartholomew boar-pig, when will thou leave fighting a' days and foining a' nights, and begin to patch up thine old body for heaven?" (II. iv. 231–3).

In his representations of Mistress Quickly and Doll Tearsheet, Shakespeare offers us a comic, parodic view of the disorderly lives of the underclass in Renaissance London. Furthermore, it is easy for us to consider the characters of the tavern *collectively*, as a satiric counterpoint to the historical main plot. In this context Pistol and Falstaff are the obvious and direct anti-heroic foils to Hal and Hotspur as well as to the plays' investment in the notion of heroism, while the lives of Quickly and Tearsheet seem to be in *excess* of the historical events and the ideological struggle over the issues of kingly authority and male power. Finally, the question still remains as to why these figures were included in the tavern scenes. To this I would respond that while many "common-sense" interpretations focus only on these scenes' comic function, feminist reading strategies that reveal the economic conditions of the prostitutes' representations can subvert and rise above the supposedly trivilizing comic intentions of the playwright.

Jean Howard, for instance, in an useful analysis of the *Henriad*, offers another feminist reading as follows:

> the tavern world . . . [in Part 2] rendered as a sexualized scene of female entreneurship, becomes the locus for the play's anxiety about a seemingly anarchic lawlessness. [Here] the sexually independent woman and the eco-nomically independent woman form a threatening combination: a challenge both to gender hierarchy and to the system of social stratification distin-guishing man from man . . . [Because of the threat they pose] their punish-ment is severe . . . unlike Falstaff, they are not just banished from the king's presence; they are carted off to be imprisoned and whipped. (14)

While her account of the way in which Mistress Quickly exerts economic control and gains some degree of economic independence in the tavern in Part 2 is very persuasive, the issue of the prostitutes' sexual independence, both in the plays and in the culture, is more problematic. Howard chooses not to "sentimentalize prostitution 'outside' patriarchy"; "the prostitute Doll's sexuality," she argues, "is not the exclusive enclosure of any one man . . . she uses men's sexual desire for her profit. When Doll is carted off at play's end, what is partly being acted out is the violent reimposition of patriarchal control over female sexuality" (11). Here, and in any discussion of prostitution, a clearer distinction needs to be made between female sexuality and desire. For whom and in what conditions does the prostitute express her sexual desire? And while she may have sexual "independence" in the brothel, at what physical cost to her body and mind? Both the dramatic and cultural texts of the Renaissance remind us that sexuality and disease coexisted in the world of the brothel.

Finally, however, I do not mean to suggest that Mistress Quickly and Doll Tearsheet are "real" women through whom we can gain unmediated access to the "experiences" of the actual prostitutes of the time, even though the Boar's Head tavern stereotypes the numerous inns in Southwark that provided cover for the flourishing prostitution trade. How-ever, in the images of the brothel, we can find textualized traces of other cultural representations of prostitutes in social and literary texts of the period, ranging from numerous city comedies to diatribes against the trade by Stubbes. Renaissance boy actors playing the parts of Mistress Quickly and Doll Tearsheet would have been familiar with the stock of stereotypical cultural images of such women. In dramatizing the tavern scenes in *1* and *2 Henry IV* Shakespeare draws on the humorous tradition and the historical settings of Southwark, rather than on the dogmatically moral perspectives of his contemporaries such as Stubbes. Thus Mistress Quickly and Doll are dramatically appealing figures who draw our empathy as they entertain us in the comic subplot. However, precisely because we find the prostitutes entertaining, there is a danger that performances that stress only the *parodic* function of the tavern scenes can downplay any consideration of the social and economic conditions of Renaissance prostitutes' lives.

Measure for Measure

In *Measure for Measure*, the green world of the earlier high comedies is shrunk into "Mariana's moated grange" and, instead of being able to escape into a vital, metamorphic space, the characters must straddle radically different places: the nunnery, the brothel, and the prison. Clearly, then, the psychic divisions between licence and restraint experienced by the characters is enacted in the split locations. Throughout the play, the supposedly Godlike Duke crosses these boundaries, while maintaining his own and their separateness intact.[33] In the last scene, as Janet Adelman has suggested, the Duke moves the plot outside the city walls, but instead of breaking down the psychic rigidity that entraps the main characters, he only reconstitutes the boundaries through a "coercion of desire" and a "distrust of sexuality" that resonate throughout the play.[34]

Even traditional, "common-sense" readings of *Measure for Measure* acknowledge that the play defies generic expectations of comedy and presents a "problem." Among these responses, there is also an impulse to fix the moral meaning of the play in terms of Christian theology, for instance, often by justifying the role and motivations of the Duke.[35] On the other extreme are feminist readings such as McLuskie's which suggest that

Feminist criticism of this play is restricted to exposing its own exclusion from the text. It has no point of entry into it, for the dilemmas of the narrative and the sexuality under discussion are constructed in completely male terms – gelding and splaying hold no terror for women – and the women's role as the objects of exchange within that system of sexuality is not at issue, however much a feminist might want to draw attention to it.[36]

A feminist reading can, I believe, engage with and intervene in the "ideological struggle over sexuality and sexual relations" which informs the text – and which reemerges in significant terms in the present.[37] One approach to this task would be via the brothel – the site of a commodified sexuality tainted by disease and despair even as it is a source of raucous bawdry and humor.

Recent, political readings of *Measure for Measure* draw our attention to the subversive aspects of the "low-life" scenes, the comic vitality of these characters and "their anarchic resistance to the due processes of law."[38] In this context, Jonathan Dollimore correctly observes that diatribes against promiscuity in the play and in the culture are expressions of an official ideology of order that displaces corruption downward onto the marginalized classes in order to relegitimate its power.[39] While Dollimore reveals the ideological underpinnings of the Duke's vision of control – which has its analogue in official theories of order in Renaissance England – he occludes an important contestatory voice in the play, that of Mistress Overdone. According to him, "the prostitutes, the most exploited group in the society which the play represents, are absent from it. . . . Looking for evidence of resistance, we find rather further evidence of exploitation" (86). Few would disagree that the prostitutes are among the most exploited and that they disappear at the end of the play. But I would like to show how Mistress Overdone narrates the story of their struggle in terms that reveal the Duke's version of an ordered history as obviously partial and oppressive. Mistress Overdone does not embody or articulate the authentic "experience" of an individual prostitute; nor do we have much sense of her as a realistic persona – a complex embodiment of a "real" person. What is important is that she reveals how the practice of prostitution in Shakespeare's Vienna – and in the Renaissance – is not an abstract moral evil, as the Duke defines it, but is determined by social, political, and economic factors within a specific historical moment.

Let us begin with the Duke's version of history: it assigns specific ideological positions to his subjects within a plan of moral renovation that is both sexually and politically oppressive. Explaining his scheme to the friar in Act I, scene iii, the Duke gives *his* account of the recent past:

We have strict statutes and most biting laws
(The needful bits and curbs to headstrong weeds)
Which for this fourteen years we have let slip,
Even like an o'ergrown lion in a cave,
That goes not out to prey. Now, as fond fathers,
Having bound up the threat'ning twigs of birch,
Only to stick it in their children's sight
For terror, not to use, in time the rod
[Becomes] more mock'd then fear'd; so our decrees,
Dead to infliction, to themselves are dead,
And liberty plucks justice by the nose;
The baby beats the nurse, and quite athwart
Goes all decorum.

(I. iii. 19–31)

The protagonist in this narrative is clearly an absolutist state in a paternalistic guise; and the history of the past "fourteen years" is represented as a law and order problem – or a period of slackening morals which pose a threat to the "natural" order and, specifically, to the hierarchy separating a paternal ruler and his "children." The Duke's account reads like a picturesque fable in which law and authority, even in the quise of an "overgrown lion," seem benign and indulgent, while the disobedient subject is represented as a disturbingly willful "baby [who] beats the nurse." What is conspicuous by its absence in his discourse is the image of the actual sites of repression, the gloomy prison and the decrepit brothel, which cast their shadow over the play. Clearly then, the Duke attempts to offer a seamless account of history, drawing a linear model that implies a continuity between the perfectly ordered past – before the subjects became disorderly – and a projected future of a renewal of order and control; thus his mode of reading typifies an elitist historiography that displaces the material facts about domination and resistance into a benevolent scheme of governing childlike subjects.

In Act I, scene ii we meet Mistress Overdone, the aging bawd, the mistress of a brothel, clearly engaged in prostitution herself – as is apparent from Pompey's many quibbles on her name. We also learn (in Act II, scene i) from Pompey's account that she is possibly a "widow" with the distinction of "nine" seemingly dubious "husbands." Other than that she has no personal history, and functions as a stock figure of ridicule and laughter in the "low-life" subplot, often mocked as a site of corruption where people "purchase" "many diseases;" her obviously precarious existence is brought to light by Pompey's telling remark: "You that have worn your eyes almost out in the service" (I. ii. 110).

Given the bawd's marginal position in the play – and in the culture – it is curious that she offers a materialist version of the history of social conditions in Duke Vicentio's Vienna, and perhaps, by inference, in Shakespeare's England, which she reveals in her complaint about her life: "Thus what with the war, what with the sweat, what with the gallows, and what with poverty, I am custom shrunk" (I. ii. 82–4). Her account is verified by Dollimore who, drawing on historians, links it to events in the winter of 1603–4: "the continuance of the war with Spain, the treason trials and executions in Winchester, the slackness of trade in the capital" (76), conditions to which one could add (as has been described earlier) the general social phenomena of growing numbers of poor and indigent during the economic and social displacements of the period. Closely following this account of struggle, we hear Mistress Overdone's plaintive cry, "What shall become of me?" Her worry – which also implies an anxiety about age and the "sweat" – does not, however, offer an isolated, individual heartbreak story; rather she seems to express a *generalized* concern and awareness of the profession of prostitution as being one of demand and supply. Thus on hearing of the edict against brothels, she asks Pompey: "what will become of those in the city?" Clearly, she is a participant in the struggle of all "unruly elements" who face the threat of being deprived of their livelihood and/or of being "geld[ed] and splay[ed]" (II. i. 230–1).

According to Ruth Mazo Karras's study of prostitution in late medieval England, our only information about prostitution comes from records on the regulation of the trade. These records show that prostitutes were tolerated, though controlled and stigmatized because of the ideology that represented "women's sexual activity as a threat to the social order and a defilement of the woman herself" (426). The prostitutes left no trace of their voices in the records of official historiography of the Renaissance. In *Measure for Measure* itself, the Duke's representations control the dramatic plot of the play as well as the narrative of authoritarian history in which he wishes to inscribe the city. The prostitutes are constituted as the marginalized or absent subjects in his discourse and they do not appear in the play's "happy" ending in which sexuality is contained within multiple marriages, even though there is the obvious ambiguity of Isabella's response to the Duke's proposal. Furthermore, Kate Keepdown, who is textually represented at the conclusion, is in many productions missing from the stage.

Mistress Overdone's exclusion is in keeping with the generic logic of the play, but nonetheless her discourse of the *commodification of female sexuality* disrupts the dominant discourse of sexual morality with its strong biblical undertones. If we center our judgment of events in the play on Overdone's perspective, then we can also see an implicit parallel between the commercialization of women in the brothel and the economic impediments to Juliet's and Mariana's marriages. Both women are social outcasts, Juliet being labelled as "immoral," because a delay or loss of a dowry prevents her from marrying the man to whom she is betrothed. In the case of Mariana, when she lost her fortune and her brother, the "moral" Angelo "Left her in tears . . . swallow'd his vows whole, pretending in her discoveries of dishonour" (III. i. 225–7). While the Duke wants to restore Mariana's status through the bed-trick, neither he, nor any other character, questions the *commercial* aspects of the marriage contract. Instead, he simply wishes to naturalize an ideology of sexual – and political – repression, under the guise of moral renovation.

Not only Mistress Overdone but, ironically enough, Angelo too exposes the contradictions within the Duke's law, though he does so through his own behavior. But it is left to the denizens of the brothel, Pompey and Overdone, to *articulate* the implicit failure of the Duke's scheme of moral renovation, no doubt reminding the London playgoers of the teeming stews of Southwark and Bankside and of the authorities' failure to shut them down permanently. Some members of the audience probably saw a correspondence between Angelo's proclamation closing the brothels and Henry VIII's "final" edict in 1546. "Though the play was written sixty years later, the event was still remembered and received literary treatment by other hands in the early seventeenth century" (Shugg, 303). Contemporary audiences probably also recalled how most civil and ecclesistical efforts at abolishing the Southwark brothels were never successful, as Pompey humorously describes a common strategy of survival: "Come; fear not you; [he tells Overdone] . . . Though you change your place, you need not change your trade" (I. ii. 106–8).

Thus the play's – and the Duke's – preoccupation with sexual constraint does not make it a universal morality tale set in the Renaissance, but rather it offers a more multifaceted view of the *historical* and *ideological* underpinnings of the sexual conflicts in the play. However, the critical history of

Measure for Measure, perhaps until recently, reveals the critics' abiding interest in psychologizing the main characters as "real" people experiencing moral and psychic divisions.[40] But of course, the stereotypical figure of Mistress Overdone cannot be read in psychoanalytic terms which ascribe to her an interiorized "self." Rather, and more importantly, she reveals to us the socio-economic as opposed to the psychological dimensions of sexuality. In this sense she is a feminist historiographer, displaying how gender and class identities produced by the practice of prostitution have little to do with "morality" but a great deal to do with the material exigencies of our lives.

Othello

To label *Othello* a "tragedy of jealousy" has almost become a critical commonplace. What has less frequently been specified is a crucial aspect of this male jealousy – namely, the fear that wives can turn into whores or, put another way, that wives and whores are indistinguishable. Iago is the most blatant spokesman of this view when, for instance, he mocks Emilia: "Come on, come on; you [women] are pictures out [a' doors] / . . . Wildcats in your kitchens, / Saints in your injuries, . . . / Players in your huswifery, and huswives in your beds" (II. i. 109–12). Wives, in Iago's view, simply keep appearances of respectability, while in fact they are "huswives" or hussies in their behavior. Thus, quite conveniently, his own fantasy of his wife's sexual infidelity with Othello is reinforced by his paranoia about unrestrained female sexuality:

> I hate the Moor,
> And it is thought abroad that 'twixt my sheets
> H'as done my office. I know not if't be true,
> But for mere suspicion in that kind,
> Will do as if for surety.
>
> (I. iii. 386–9)

The fear and horror of female sexuality that permeate Renaissance discourses about women serve as a useful resource for Iago to plant suspicion in Othello's mind. Although the play's conclusion restores "both Desdemona'a idealized chastity and Othello's idealized masculinity," the ironies of this "moral" resolution are manifold.[41] Consistently, Desdemona has little difficulty in defining her identity as a faithful wife as distinguished from a whore: "I cannot say "whore,". / It does abhor me now I speak the word;" (IV. ii. 161–2). However, in the fantasy of dishonor brought to life by Iago, Othello's masculine honor can only be "saved" by marking Desdemona, as the representative of all woman, as a "whore." Even her own father, Brabantio, mistrusts her fidelity, as he warns the Moor, "She has deceiv'd her father, and may thee" (I. iii. 293). She defies her father to follow her own desire and is punished for it. What is at stake in her defiance is the fact that women were not allowed to be desiring subjects within the reigning gender ideology of Shakespeare's Venice – and of Renaissance England.

Feminist readings of *Othello* – ranging from Newman to Adelman – all illustrate the misogynistic cultural images of female sexuality in the Renaissance.[42] In the eyes of the men in the play, ideal femininity is threatened by the monstrous desires of women, as Othello laments. "O curse of marriage, / That we can call these delicate creatures ours, / And not their appetites!" (III. iii. 268–70). While the male characters assert a dichotomy between women's identities as ideal objects of desire (wives) and desiring subjects (whores), the play itself displaces this simple division, thus opening up a space for a feminist reading that intervenes in the ideological struggle over female sexuality that informs the plot.

A useful way of reading this struggle would be to foreground Bianca's role, specifically as it reveals the contradictions within the simple dichotomy between wives and whores. In the eyes of the male characters Bianca is a "courtesan," supposedly the only "real" whore among the women characters. All men, ranging from Iago to Cassio, view her as a common prostitute: for instance, Iago introduces her by defining the material conditions of her existence: "A huswife that by selling her desires / Buys herself bread and [clothes]. It is a creature / That dotes on Cassio (as 'tis the strumpet's plague / To beguile many and be beguiled by one (IV. i. 94–7). The subsequent exchange between him and Cassio reinforces Bianca's identity as an object of mockery, while unwittingly revealing her to be a woman of feeling and loyalty rather than an embodiment of a "monstrous" and commodified female desire.

Cassio: Alas, poor rogue, I think, [i' faith], she loves me.
Iago: She gives it out that you shall marry her. Do you intend it? . . .

Cassio: I marry [her]! What? a customer! . . . She is persuaded I will marry her,
out of her own love and flattery, not out of my promise . . . She was here
even now; she haunts me in every place . . . She hangs, and lolls, and
weeps upon me.

(IV. i. 111–40)

One critic persuasively states that "Bianca's active, open-eyed enduring
affection is similar to that of the other women. She neither romanticizes
love nor degrades sex."[43] This description certainly fits Bianca's insistent
pursuit of Cassio. In fact, her spontaneous desire for Cassio is no different
from Desdemona's for Othello, as when she declares her feelings at being
parted from her lover: "What? keep a week away? / seven days and seven
nights? / . . . and lovers' absent hours, / . . . O weary reckoning" (III. iv.
173–6). However, even if the play offers little evidence of Bianca's sexual
availability to all men, she must be cast as a whore in order to serve as an
embodiment of Desdemona's transgression, as Othello imagines it.[44] She is
made to play the harlot in Iago's plot as a means of incriminating
Desdemona by enacting the "proof" of the latter's infidelity.

Jonathan Dollimore discusses the play in the context of a series of
"displacements, one being that the "perverse subject the desiring woman
[Desdemona] – becomes through imagined sexual transgression, a surrogate alien, a surrogate Turk," threatening "country, race, and class" (*Sexual
Dissidence*, 155–6). While showing how the demonization of Desdemona is
important to the sexual and moral economy of the play, Dollimore, however, omits Bianca's crucial role in the production of Desdemona as a
"whore." It is interesting to note that in Cinthio's original novella,
Hecatommithi, the handkerchief-copier is not the same person as the harlot,
and one cannot conjecture at Shakespeare's intentions in making this
switch (Colman, 123). However, by making Bianca, the composite of the
two characters (and giving her the handkerchief), Shakespeare makes it
easier for Iago to produce "ocular proof" of Desdemona's adultery, while
insidiously suggesting an identity between Bianca and Desdemona.

I do not mean to idealize Bianca or to gloss over her socially defined
identity as a courtesan, if not a common prostitute. She is of course a minor
character in both Shakespeare's and Iago's scheme of things, and her a role
is a function of the dramatic plot – as a recipient of the handkerchief and
a convenient foil to Desdemona. If female desire is, as the men see it, fearful
and monstrous, Bianca, like Desdemona, hardly seems to embody any

threat. It is left to Emilia to define women's roles as desiring subjects: "Let husbands know / Their wives have sense like them; they . . . have their palates both for sweet and sour, / As husbands have" (IV. iii. 93–5). While Emilia considers the possibility of infidelity and often stirs the suspicions of her husband, ultimately her concern here, and through the play, is not so much to promote adultery as to advocate women's need to represent themselves.

At the end of the play, it is Emilia who questions Othello's suspicion of Desdemona and ironically reinforces the problematic issue of "proof." "Why should he call her whore? / Who keeps her company? / What place? What time?" (IV. ii. 137–8). Finally, however, while the play makes visible and even implicitly validates women's roles as desiring subjects, it privileges the male gaze as it constructs the fantasy of their infidelity; and in this fantasy, because women have little control over whether they will be cast as wives or whores, they have to pay dearly.

Bianca has had to "pay dearly" in terms of the editorial history of *Othello* in that she is literally assigned a sexual status in the cast of characters that *preface* most modern editions of the play. Most often Bianca is labelled a "courtezan," as for instance, in the *Riverside* edition of the complete works of Shakespeare. Going back to the manuscripts of the Quarto versions (1622 and 1630), one does not find any list of characters appended at the beginning or the end of the play. Bianca is described as a "curtezan" in the First Folio (1623), though the cast of characters is listed at the *end* of the play, rather than in a preface. Since then there have been some seemingly minor yet telling deviations from this practice, as in a 1681 edition when she is called "Cassio's Wench." Later, in a 1755 edition, she is described as Bianca, "a Courtezan, mistress to Cassio, and in an 1895 version, she is simply assigned the role of "Cassio's mistress," a title that is repeated in the 1960 Cambridge edition. Most recently, Wells and Taylor offer another, frequently used compromise by describing Bianca as a " 'curtezan', in love with Cassio."[45]

These variations may seem like irrelevant quibbles in terms of Bianca's identity, but they are in effect crucial in determining whether she is, after all, a "whore," a common prostitute who sells her sexual attentions to *all* men. In an editorial comment that prefaces the Arden edition (1962), M. R. Ridley briefly mentions the import of the various editorial choices: "I [Ridley] have retained the F's description of Bianca [i.e., as 'Curtezan'] since the usual 'Mistress to Cassio' implies a more permanent relationship than is anywhere implied in the text, except (possibly) in one disputed line."[46] Of course Ridley is right in suggesting that Iago's opening reference to Cassio as a "fellow almost damn'd in a fair wife," (I. i. 21) is ambiguous at best. At this point, and throughout the play, we know very little of the origins of Cassio's relationship with Bianca. However, M. R. Ridley and others simply replicate the received editorial tradition, assuming that Bianca is a courtesan, who is sexually available to *any* man, simply because she is *not a wife*. Here, I am not suggesting that editors should ignore the "proof" of the First Folio, but simply that Bianca's *behavior* in the play offers no evidence to suggest that she has or will provide sexual favors to other men, hence, perhaps, the less judgmental decision of some editors to call her "Cassio's Mistress." But once an editor assigns the label of "courtesan" to Bianca, her ardent devotion to Cassio as his loyal "mistress" is seen in a different light, and we may overlook her loyalty, which in a wife as in Desdemona would be considered praiseworthy.

A brief look at this editorial history shows us how critical and editorial traditions are complicit with assigning sexual roles to female characters in ways that replicate the ideologies of the male characters within the plays. One can find an instance of such a complicity in Granville Barker's description in *Prefaces to Shakespeare*: "In . . . place of [the Captain's wife in the original source, Shakespeare] conjured out of a single phrase in the story concerning a courtesan he [Cassio] was about to visit, we have Bianca whose fraility, with its affectations of virtue, is set against Desdemona's innate chastity . . ."(5). Once again, the critic falls back on a neat distinction between chaste wives and other women who supposedly lack virtue because their sexuality is not contained in marriage. In the plot of the play, we find little cause to believe that Bianca's devotion to Cassio is an "affectation." Rather, she consistently seeks Cassio's love (and at least implicitly on a permanent basis), but cannot do so as long as she remains trapped in the category of "courtesan" or "whore" imposed on her by her critics both within and beyond the play.

This story of prostitutes and courtesans in Renaissance literary and cultural texts has not been a simple task of making visible the experiences of individual women. Instead, I have attempted to read against the grain of standard generic, critical, and moral conventions by which prostitutes were represented by the humanists, civic authorities, cultural historians, and literary critics. From this approach there emerges a complex relation between the economic practice of prostitution and the masculine fear of female sexuality. As feminists, when we try to unravel the complicated strands of discourses in which categories such as "woman" and "harlot" are entangled, we have to make an effort to go beyond the moralizing intent of many descriptions of women's roles as "wives" and "whores." Thus the power of the discursive becomes quite apparent in ideologically holding in place a gender system which erased the fact that sexual transactions between men and women – in and out of marriage – were mediated by other, material determinations. As feminists, then, as we examine the gender struggle in Renaissance society – and in the present – we must recognize and make visible how women were and are *assigned* fixed and "natural" roles in society, even though their experiences are constituted by social and material forces. Thus, when Emilia questions why Othello must call Desdemona "whore," her voice is lost in the male drama of jealousy and a fear of cuckoldry. Our role as feminist historians and literary critics is not simply to recover her voice – to speak for her, so to speak – but more importantly, to disrupt *the categories of representation* accepted by Othello, Iago, Cassio, and others, and that in different manifestations continue to oppress women today.

Notes

My thanks to Mark Burnett and Miranda Chaytor for their comments and suggestions, which greatly improved the final version of this essay. I also appreciate Jennifer Holland's and Lashonda Watson's prompt and innovative research assistance.

All quotations from Shakespeare's plays are taken from the Riverside edition, ed. G. Blakemore Evans (Boston, Houghton Mifflin, 1974). I have also consulted the following editions: *The Tragoedy of Othello*, First and Second Quartos, London, 1622 and 1630 (*STC* 22305 and 22306), Huntington Library MSS; *Othello* in the *First Folio* (1623), Norton facsimile, ed. Charlton Hinman (New York, W. W. Norton, 1968); *Othello, The Moor of Venice*, 1681 (another Quarto), facsimile edition (London, Cornmarket Press, 1969); *Othello* (1755), facsimile edition (London, Cornmarket Press, 1969); *Shakespeare's Tragedy of Othello*, ed. Israel Gollancz (London, Dent, 1895); *Othello*, ed. Alice Walker and John Dover Wilson (Cambridge, Cambridge University Press, 1960); *Othello* in *The Complete Works of Shakespeare*, ed. Stanley Wells and Gary Taylor (Oxford, Clarendon Press, 1986); the Arden edition of *The Works of William Shakespeare*, ed. M. R. Ridley (Cambridge, MA, Methuen, 1962).

1 See Gayle Green and Coppélia Kahn's introduction to *Making A Difference*: *Feminist Literary Criticism*, 12–28. They read Isak Dinesen's tale "The Blank Page" as a paradigm for a feminist historiography that must make "the silences speak" (13).

2 See Hayden White's analysis of Foucault's methodology in "Foucault decoded," in *Tropics of Discourse*, 230–40.

3 For details of Scott's theory of gender, read "Gender."

4 I am indebted to Tony Bennett's discussion of the relation between the discursive and the social in "Texts in history," 78–9.

5 Various aspects of the social changes of the period, as well as of the disruptions in the ideology of order and degree are discussed in Underdown, 9–43, and Wrightson, 17–38. Note also Newman, 91–3, who focuses on the contradictions in the gender ideology of the period; and Archer, 1–17.

6 See Natalie Davis's essay, "Women on top," in *Society and Culture in Early Modern France*, 124–51.

7 James Scott, in *Domination and the Arts of Resistance*, 17–44, offers a provocative theory of resistance by which he distinguishes between public transcripts, "the self-portrait of the dominant elites" (18) and hidden transcripts of the subordinate groups, which are "disguised forms of public dissent" (20).

8 Mary Beth Rose, "Introduction" to *Women in the Middle Ages and the Renaissance*, xiv.

9 See Kathleen McLuskie's *Renaissance Dramatists*, especially the way in which she theorizes the difficulties of writing a feminist history, 224–30. Also relevant is Belsey's formulation of a dialectical historiography in *The Subject of Tragedy*, 1–54.

10 For a detailed account of the relation between history and experience, see Joan Scott, "The Evidence of Experience."

11 I am indebted to Scott's essay, "The Evidence of Experience," 778, for her discussion of experience and categories of representation. Also applicable is Spivak, 790–4.

12 McLuskie, in *Renaissance Dramatists*, discusses different approaches to reading women's resistance in the Renaissance, 225–7.

13 Ian Archer's analysis of "crime and society" in Elizabethan London, 204–56, explains how brothels were seen as promoting social instability because they harboured apprentices and masterless vagrants. Paul Griffiths, 40–3, makes further connections between the regulation of brothels and an unease about possible social disruption. Also see Shugg, 291–306.

14 Archer, 207.

15 Both Archer, 204–6, and Shugg, 305–6, show that a complete suppression of prostitution was impossible, especially in the suburbs that were not under the Lord Mayor.

16 See the arguments of Thomas Becon's *Homely agaynst whordom*, which is structured by this dichotomy between "wives" and "whores."

17 For a full account of the early Church Fathers' view, see Jordan, 25–9. Also see Schulenburg, 31–2, for a discussion of the early Church Fathers' warnings against female sexuality. My thanks to Valerie Wayne for her comments on this section of the chapter.

18 See Woodbridge for the controversial debates regarding the "nature" of woman, 152–83. "Defences" of women inevitably stressed virtue and self-sacrifice as two important qualities for women.

19 See Gosonhyll's references to biblical stereotypes of female virtue in his defence of women in *Mulierum Paean* in Henderson and McManus, 156–70.

20 Frances and Joseph Gies, 57–8 discuss Gratian's views on the reform of prostitutes through marriage.

21 See Callaghan's discussion of subjectivity and desire, this volume, ch. 2. Her subtle analysis of this topic has greatly deepened my understanding of it.

22 See "The debate about women," in Henderson and McManus, 3–46.

23 Related themes are echoed in popular ballads of the period, such as in Rollins (ed.), *A Gorgeous Gallery of Gallant Inventions* (1578), 8–18.

24 For a useful reading of Greene's *The Conversion of an English Courtizen*, see McLuskie, " 'Lawless desires well tempered'," 106–10.

25 Arthur Kinney aptly uses this term to describe the social displacements of the period. He offers a vivid picture of the teeming masses of vagrants and poor in Renaissance England, 11–57.

26 A. L. Beier examines at length the reasons for growing numbers of vagrants and unemployed in early modern England, 14–28. He shows that structural changes in agriculture production dispossessed large numbers of smallholders from their land, transforming them into struggling wage-workers, with little scope for upward mobility.

27 Among plays that offer the solution of providing husbands for whores are *A Trick to Catch the Old One* (Middleton), *A Mad World, My Masters* (Middleton), and *The Woman Hater* (Beaumont).

28 Rackin makes a persuasive case for the way in which hetereogenous voices disrupt the historiographic tradition in the history plays, 222–34.

29 Rackin's reading of Falstaff's subversive role, 234–40, is echoed by other critics such as Bristol in *Carnival and Theatre*, 204–6.

30 A number of critics including Bristol, 197–206, draw on Bakhtin's notion of the subversive role of carnival in *Rabelais and His World* to describe the Eastcheap scenes.

31 For a discussion of Mistress Quickly, see Rackin, 245–6.

32 Bawds or keepers of brothels sometimes had husbands or "protectors" who gave them a quasi-respectable status. Some women could even refer to

themselves as "widows" for the sake of respectablity.

33 See Janet Adelman's account of the physical and psychic divisions in *Measure for Measure*, 99–100.

34 Adelman, 97–100.

35 A number of critics stress the play's unifying Christian themes without seeing this as a "problem." Among these are Hunter, Battenhouse, and Lever, "The Disguised Ruler," in which the Duke is described as "a model ruler for a Christian polity" (25). Also relevant is G. Wilson Knight's "*Measure for Measure* and the Gospels."

36 For a perceptive analysis of the "problem" posed by this play for feminists, see McLuskie's "The patriarchal bard," 97–8.

37 While McLuskie in "The patriarchal bard," 97, sees few possibilities for a feminist reading of this play, I find that the play's treatment of prevailing sexual ideologies very useful for a feminist analysis.

38 McLuskie, in "The patriarchal bard," 93, briefly discusses the "low-life" characters, but does not elaborate on the brothel scenes.

39 Dollimore's reading of "transgression and surveillance" in *Measure for Measure* is an important materialist analysis of the way in which sexual ideologies perpetuate class differences.

40 Janet Adelman's psychoanalytic reading is a good instance of such approaches.

41 For a fuller account of such ironies in *Othello*, see Adelman, 71.

42 See Newman's reading of the Renaissance fear of "monstrous" femininity, 116–43.

43 Carol Thomas Neely's essay, "Women and Men in *Othello*," offers a useful discussion of Bianca's character, 218–19.

44 I am indebted to Newman (see n. 42) for this reading of Bianca's role.

45 The editions I have referred to are listed in the introductory note.

46 See Ridley's brief note and introduction to *Othello* in the Arden edition.

Works Cited

Adelman, Janet, *Suffocating Mothers: Fantasies of Maternal Origin in Shakespeare's Plays* (London, Routledge, 1992).

Amussen, Susan Dwyer, *An Ordered Society: Gender and Class in Early Modern England* (Oxford, Basil Blackwell, 1988).

Archer, Ian W., *The Pursuit of Stability: Social Relations in Elizabethan London* (Cambridge, Cambridge University Press, 1991).

Aydelotte, Frank (ed.), *Elizabethan Rogues and Vagabonds* (Oxford, Clarendon Press, 1913).

Baker, Herschel, "Introduction to *Henry IV 1–2*," *The Riverside Shakespeare* (Boston, Houghton Mifflin, 1974), 842–6.

Battenhouse, Roy, "*Measure for Measure* and the Christian doctrine of atonement," *PMLA*, 61 (1946), 1029–59.

Becon, Thomas, *The Works of Thomas Becon, vol. II. London: 1560. (STC* 1710).

Beier, A. L., *Masterless Men: The Vagrancy Problem in England, 1560–1640* (London, Methuen, 1985).

Belsey, Catherine, *The Subject of Tragedy: Identity and Difference in Renaissance Drama* (London, Methuen, 1985).

Bennett, Tony, "Texts in history: the determinations of readings and their texts," in Derek Attridge et al. (eds), *Poststructuralism and the Question of History* (Cambridge, Cambridge University Press, 1989).

Berlin, Norman, *The Base String: The Underworld in Elizabethan Drama* (Teaneck, NJ, Fairleigh Dickinson University Press, 1968).

Bridenbaugh, Carl, *Vexed and Troubled Englishmen, 1590–1642* (Oxford, Oxford University Press, 1968).

Bristol, Michael, *Carnival and Theatre: Plebeian Culture and the Structure of Authority in Renaissance England* (London, Routledge, 1985).

Burford, E. J., *Bawds and Lodgings: A History of the London Bankside Brothels – 1600–1675* (London, Peter Owen, 1976).

Burnett, Mark Thornton, "Calling 'things by their right names': troping prostitution, politics and *The Dutch Courtesan*," unpublished paper.

Cahn, Susan, *Industry of Devotion: The Transformation of Women's Work in England, 1500–1660* (New York, Columbia University Press, 1987).

Clark, Alice, *Working Life of Women in the Seventeenth Century* (New York, Harcourt & Brace, 1920).

Colman, E. A. M., *The Dramatic Use of Bawdy in Shakespeare* (London, Longman, 1974).

Davis, Natalie Zemon, "Women on top," in *Society and Culture in Early Modern France* (Stanford, Stanford University Press, 1975), 124–51.

Dollimore, Jonathan, "Transgression and surveillance in *Measure for Measure*," in Jonathan Dollimore and Alan Sinfield (eds), *Political Shakespeare: New Essays in Cultural Materialism* (Ithaca, Cornell University Press, 1985), 72–87.

——, *Sexual Dissidence: Augustine to Wilde, Freud to Foucault* (Oxford, Clarendon Press, 1991).

Erasmus, Desiderius, "A pithy Dialogue between a Harlot and a godly yong man" (1523), in *Utile Dulce: Or Trueths Libertie*, trans. William Burton (1606) (New York and Amsterdam: Da Capo Press, 1973).

Ferguson, Margaret W., Quilligan, Maureen, and Vickers, Nancy (eds), *Rewriting the Renaissance: The Discourses of Sexual Difference in Early Modern Europe* (Chicago, University of Chicago Press, 1986).

56   Jyotsna Singh

Foucault, Michel, *Power/Knowledge: Selected Interviews* (New York, Pantheon Books, 1972).

Furnivall, Frederick J. (ed.), *Harrison's Description of England in Shakespere's Youth* (1577–87), 2nd and 3rd books (London, Trubner, 1877).

Gies, Frances, and Joseph Gies, *Women in the Middle Ages* (New York, Harper & Row, 1978).

Gouda, Francis, "Men's fantasies, women's realities" (review of Charles Bernheimer, *Figures of Ill Repute: Representing Prostitution in Nineteenth-Century France* and Alain Corbin, *Women for Hire: Prostitution and Sexuality in France after 1850*), *The Women's Review of Books*, September 14, 1990, 13–14.

Granville-Barker, Harley, *Prefaces to Shakespeare*, vol. II (London, Batsford, 1972).

Greene, Gayle and Kahn, Coppélia (eds), *Making a Difference: Feminist Literary Criticism* (London, Methuen, 1985).

Greene, Robert, "The Conversion of an English Courtizan" (1592), in *The Life and Complete Works of Robert Greene*, vol. x, ed. Alexander Grosart (New York, Russell & Russell, 1964), 237–76.

Griffiths, Paul, "The structure of prostitution in Elizabethan London," *Continuity and Change*, 8(I) (1993), 39–63.

Henderson, Katherine Usher, and McManus, Barbara F. (eds), *Half Humankind: Contexts and Texts about the Controversy about Women in England, 1540–1640* (Urbana, University of Illinois Press, 1985).

Hageman, Elizabeth H., review of Margaret Ferguson, Maureen Quilligan, and Nancy J. Vickers (eds), *Rewriting the Renaissance: The Discourses of Sexual Difference in Early Modern Europe*, and Mary Beth Rose (ed.), *Women in the Middle Ages and the Renaissance: Literary and Historical Perspectives, Shakespeare Quarterly*, 39 (1988), 247–51.

Haselkorn, Anne, *Prostitution in Elizabethan and Jacobean Comedy* (Troy, NY, Whitston, 1983).

Hedrick, Donald K., "Dead hostages: historiography at a disadvantage in *Henry V*," paper presented at the Shakespeare Association of America, Boston, 1988.

Howard, Jean E., "Forming the Commonwealth: Including, Excluding, and Criminalizing women in Heywood's *Edward IV* and Shakespeare's *Henry IV*," unpublished paper.

Hunter, Robert, *Shakespeare and the Comedy of Forgiveness* (New York, Columbia University Press, 1965).

Jordan, Constance, *Renaissance Feminism: Literary Texts and Political Models* (Ithaca, Cornell University Press, 1990).

Karras, Ruth Mazo, "The Regulation of Brothels in Later Medieval England," *Signs* (winter 1989), 399–433.

Kelso, Ruth, *Doctrine for the Lady of the Renaissance* (Urbana, University of Illinois Press, 1978).

Kinney, Arthur (ed.), *Rogues, Vagabonds, and Sturdy Beggars* (Amherst, University of Massachusetts Press, 1990).

Latimer, Hugh, *Sermons of Bishop Hugh Latimer*, ed. G. E. Corrie, Parker Society, vol. XXII (1844).

Lever, J. W., "The Disguised Ruler," in George C. Geckle (ed.), *Twentieth Century Interpretations of "Measure for Measure"* (Englewood Cliffs, NJ, Prentice-Hall, 1970), 21–6.

MacLean, Ian, *The Renaissance Notion of Women* (Cambridge, Cambridge, University Press, 1980).

McLuskie, Kathleen, "The patriarchal bard: feminist criticism and Shakespeare, *King Lear* and *Measure for Measure*," in Jonathan Dollimore and Alan Sinfield (eds), *Political Shakespeare* (Ithaca, Cornell University Press, 1985).

——, *Renaissance Dramatists* (Atlantic Highlands, Humanities Press, 1989).

——, " 'Lawless desires well tempered'," in Susan Zimmerman (ed.), *Erotic Politics: Desire on the Renaissance Stage* (London, Routledge, 1992).

Neely, Carol Thomas, "Women and Men in *Othello*: 'What should such a fool / Do with so good a woman?," in Carolyn Ruth Swift Lenz et al. (eds), *The Woman's Part* (Urbana, University of Illinois Press, 1980), 211–39.

——, "Constructing the Subject: Feminist Practice and New Renaissance Discourses," *English Literary Renaissance*, 18 (1988), 5–18.

Newman, Karen, "Femininity and the Monstrous in *Othello*," in Jean Howard and Marion O'Connor (eds), *Shakespeare Reproduced* (London, Routledge, 1987).

Prior, Mary (ed.), *Women in English Society, 1500–1800* (London, Methuen, 1985).

Rackin, Phyllis *Stages of History: Shakespeare's English Chronicles* (Ithaca, Cornell University Press, 1990).

Rollins, Hyder E. (ed.), *A Gorgeous Gallery of Gorgeous Inventions* (1578) (Cambridge, MA, Harvard University Press, 1926).

Rose, Mary Beth (ed.), *Women in the Middle Ages and the Renaissance: Literary and Cultural Perspectives* (Syracuse, Syracuse University Press, 1986).

Ruggiero, Guido, "Sexual criminality in early Renaissance Venice, 1338–1358," *Journal of Social History* (summer 1975), 18–37.

Salgado, Gamini, *The Elizabethan Underworld* (London, Dent, 1977).

Schulenburg, Jane Tibbets, "The heroics of virginity: brides of Christ and sacrificial mutilation," in Mary Beth Rose (ed.), *Women in the Middle Ages and the Renaissance* (Syracuse, Syracuse University Press, 1986).

Scott, James C., *Domination and the Arts of Resistance* (New Haven, Yale University Press, 1990).

Scott, Joan W., "Gender: A Useful Category of Historical Analysis," in Elizabeth Weed (ed.), *Coming to Terms: Feminism, Theory, Politics* (London, Routledge, 1989), 81–100.

——, "The Evidence of Experience," *Critical Inquiry* (summer 1991), 773–97.

Sharpe, J. A., *Early Modern England: A social History, 1550–1760* (London, Edward Arnold, 1987).

Shugg, Wallace, "Prostitution in Shakespeare's London," *Shakespeare Studies*, X (1977), 291–313.

Spivak, Gayatri Chakravarty, *In Other Worlds: Essays in Cultural Politics* (London, Routledge, 1988).

Stow, John, *A Survey of London* (1598) (London, Whittaker, 1842).

Stubbes, Philip, *The Anatomie of Abuses* (London, 1583). (*STC* 23376).

Underdown, David, *Revel, Riot, and Rebellion: Popular Politics and Culture in England* (Oxford, Clarendon Press, 1985).

White, Hayden, "Foucault decoded," in *Tropics of Discourse: Essays in Cultural Criticism* (Baltimore, Johns Hopkins University Press, 1978), 230–60.

Wiener, Carol Z., "Sex roles and crime in late Elizabethan Hertfordshire," *Journal of Social History* (summer 1975), 38–60.

Williamson, Marilyn, *The Patriarchy of Shakespeare's Comedies* (Detroit, Wayne State University Press, 1986).

Wilson Knight, G., "*Measure for Measure* and the Gospels," in George C. Geckle (ed.), *Twentieth Century Interpretations of "Measure for Measure."* (Englewood Cliffs, Prentice-Hall, 1970), 21–6.

Woodbridge, Linda, *Women and the English Renaissance: Literature and the Nature of Womankind, 1540–1620* (Urbana, University of Illinois Press, 1984).

Wrightson, Keith, *English Society, 1580–1680* (London, Hutchinson, 1982).

2

The Ideology of Romantic Love

The Case of *Romeo and Juliet*

Dympna C. Callaghan

"To this end . . . is this tragicall matter written, to describe unto thee a couple of unfortunate lovers, thralling themselves to unhonest desire, neglecting the authority and advice of parents and friends . . ." (Evans, 1057). Thus Arthur Brooke defines the ideological project of his poem, *The Tragicall History of Romeous and Juliet* (1562), which was to become Shakespeare's primary source for *Romeo and Juliet*. The lovers' "unhonest desire" was always a compelling feature of the story, but in Shakespeare's version the fate of that desire is presented as profound injustice as much as proper punishment.[1] For Brooke's rendition of the story bears a moral aversion to what Shakespeare's tragedy accomplishes in producing for posterity the lovers' desire as at once transgressive ("unhonest") and as a new orthodoxy (tragically legitimated). It is precisely this ambivalence that is at the heart of the play's appeal as one of the preeminent cultural documents of love in the West.

Romeo and Juliet was written at the historical moment when the ideologies and institutions of desire – romantic love and the family, which are now for us completely naturalized – were being negotiated. Indeed, the play consolidates a certain formation of desiring subjectivity attendant upon Protestant and especially Puritan ideologies of marriage and the family required by, or least very conducive to the emergent economic formation of, capitalism.[2] The goal of this chapter is to examine the role of *Romeo and Juliet* in the cultural construction of desire. Desire – variously generated, suppressed, unleashed, and constrained – is particularly significant for feminist cultural studies because in its most common formulation as transhistorical romantic love it is one of the most efficient and irresistible interpellations of the female subject, securing her complicity in apparently unchangeable structures of oppression, particularly compulsory heterosexuality and bourgeois marriage.

It would be wrong to suggest that romantic love is devoid of positive and even liberatory dimensions. As Denis de Rougement has shown in *Love in the Western World*, its advent in the twelfth century represents something of an improvement on earlier organizations of desire. It seems likely, however, that the extra-marital love that flourished among the feudal aristocracy was considerably less restrictive for women (though not actively empowering) than was the marital version that emerged with early capitalism. Feudal romantic love was generally constructed as the unrequited passion of a male subject leading ultimately to his own spiritual self-transcendence, as opposed to the emergent construction of romantic love as mutual heterosexual desire leading to a consummation in marriage, a union of both body and spirit. One of its crucial features, a signal of its effectiveness, is that the ideology of romantic love centers from the Renaissance onward on women's subjective experience. Yet this focus serves to control and delimit intimate experience rather than to allow the fullest possible expression of female desire. It is also true that when we are in its throes, romantic love is a classic instance of false consciousness. Among its oppressive effects, the dominant ideology of (heterosexual, monogamous) romantic love relegates homosexuality to the sphere of deviance, secures women's submission to the asymmetrical distribution of power between men and women, and bolsters individualism by positing sexual love as the expression of authentic identity. Men are not, of course, immune to these effects, but they are more likely than women to derive benefit from them. My analysis of this phenomenon proceeds first by examining the ideological function of *Romeo and Juliet* in the Renaissance and in the present, and then moves on to critique the discourses (those of psychoanalysis and history) which should enable the historicization of desire in Renaissance studies, but which in certain key respects actually impede it. Here, my approach is necessarily and deliberately synoptic because I endeavor to place desire in terms of the determinate, global conceptual categories of Marxism. The final sections of the chapter address the complex operations of desire within the play itself.

Reproducing the Ideology of Romantic Love

Shakespeare's text has been used to perpetuate the dominant ideology of romantic love, and its initial ideological function has intensified since its first performance. The play enacts an ideological propensity to posit desire as transhistorical. For what is extraordinary about the version of familial and personal relations – of desire and identity and their relation to power – endorsed by *Romeo and Juliet* is that they are in our own time so fully naturalized as to seem universal. Feminist psychoanalytic critic Julia Kristeva writes: "Young people throughout the entire world, whatever their race, religion, or social status, identify with the adolescents of Verona . . ." (210). According to Kristeva and countless Shakespeareans, the play constitutes a universal legend of love representing elemental psychic forces of desire and frustration purportedly characteristic of the human condition in every age and culture.[3]

The iteration of a particular configuration of desire does not end, therefore, in 1595 when the first performance puts it in place, but rather is a phenomenon that has been perpetuated, indeed universalized, by subsequent critical and theatrical reproductions of the play.[4] As Joseph Porter points out, *Romeo and Juliet* "has become far more canonical a story of heterosexual love than it was when it came to Shakespeare's hand" (141). Consider, for example, that in its Elizabethan production, Romeo and Juliet were portrayed not by an actor and actress but by a suitably feminine-featured male performer and a slightly more rugged youth, and that the erotic homology produced by this situation was compounded by the presence of the profoundly homoerotic Mercutio. The play's initial ideological project – the valorization of romantic love between the young couple – thus becomes consolidated and intensified with subsequent re-narrations. Indeed, the affective power of the story and of romantic love itself – its "dateless passion" (Evans et al., 1057) – occurs not in spite of its repetition but rather depends precisely on reiteration.

The narrative mechanisms of the text itself tend towards self-replication. Shakespeare's play perpetuates an already well-known tale, and Act V produces "closure" on desire only by opening up the possibility of endless retellings of the story – displacing the lovers' desire onto a perpetual narrative of love (see Whittier, 41; Jones).[5] The lovers' story is recapitulated by the prologue, by the lovers, and by the Friar. The Prince offers the concluding incitement to "more talk": "never was a story of more woe / Than this of Juliet and her Romeo" (V. iii. 307; 309–10). The play's ending thus constitutes a means of monumentalizing (quite literally in the golden statues of the lovers) and thereby reproducing *ad infinitum*, "whiles Verona by that name is known" (V. iii. 300), the ideological imperatives of the lovers' most poignant erotic moments. Crucially, then, the social

effectivity of the ideology of romantic love is characterized fundamentally
by its capacity for self-replication. Thus, the narrative imperative of *Romeo
and Juliet* to propagate the desire with which it is inscribed constitutes a
resistance to historicization that has been extended by criticism's production of the play as universal love story. In this respect, the mimetic
dynamic curiously mirrors the capitalist mode of production, whose goal is
not immediate use but accumulated and multiplied future production (see
Kamenka and Neale, 18). The play's inclination towards replication and
multiplication is a maneuver that propagates a version of erotic love which
is consonant with the needs of an emergent social order.

Romeo and Juliet, then, marks the inauguration of a particular form of
sexual desire produced in accordance with the specific historical requirements of patriarchy's shifting modality. As Eli Zaretsky argues in his
pathbreaking study *Capitalism, the Family, and Personal Life*, "courtly love
anticipated ideals of love and individualism that the bourgeois located
within the family and that were generalized and transformed in the course
of capitalist development" (38). In the early modern teleology of desire, the
family, newly emphasized as the focus of political, social, legal, and economic organization becomes the social destination of desire.[6] Thus, *Romeo
and Juliet* both instantiates the ideology of romantic love as universal,
timeless and unchanging and yet is marked by its own historical specificity. The degree to which *Romeo and Juliet* appears to constitute the tran-
scription of the universal features of the experience of love indicates its
profoundly "ideological" nature; that is to say, the play's ideological
project has become the dominant ideology of desire. In this way, the text
both positions itself within and reproduces the hegemonic. *Romeo and Juliet*
consolidates the ideology of romantic love and the correlative crystalization
of the modern nuclear family.

Disciplining Desire: Psychoanalysis and History

The tendency to posit desire as transhistorical, as we shall see, is not
confined to Shakespeare's text. Freud himself conflated psychic, social, and
historical processes, most notoriously perhaps in his account of the origins
of patriarchy in *Totem and Taboo*. Here, the primal father is overthrown and
eaten by his sons, who in their guilt, after a considerable period of time,
reinstate the father's strictures, which by now they have all too thoroughly

and literally ingested: "Each single one of the brothers who had banded together for the purposes of killing their father was inspired by a wish to become like him and had given expression to it by incorporating parts of their father's surrogate in the totem meal" (505). Posited as a fact of prehistory, this is a far more literal manifestation of the rivalry between father and son inherent in the Oedipus complex.[7] Freud also argued that we all carry a philogenetic memory of this "real" event, a claim he repeated in his last work, *Moses and Monotheism*.[8] The point here is not to add weight to the already heavy indictment against Freud; rather, what is critical is that he posited a real event as the origin of the human family, a site of the individual psychic scenario, and was himself (particularly in these texts which are examples of his speculative, as opposed to his strictly psychoanalytic writings) grappling with, or conversely evading, the problem of "real history."[9]

In contemporary critical analyses, the understanding of desire as transhistorical is similarly produced by the way psychoanalysis (the dominant critical apparatus of desire) is positioned in relation to questions of historical specificity.[10] Feminism, far from resolving this conflicted relationship, is in fact heavily invested in it. This is because, on the one hand, constructions of gender and sexuality are seen to be historically specific and, on the other, fundamental aspects of patriarchy are stubbornly tenacious – well nigh universal. The law of the father has been an apparently immutable force in psychic and social organization and is enacted in and structured by the Oedipus complex,[11] and the desire which is a necessary condition of human subjectivity comes into being under the "Law of the Father." There are always "two parents of the opposite sex and their relationship to each other and their offspring, and its to them" (Mitchell, *Woman's Estate*, 169; see also Coward, 15, and Weeks, 159). Juliet Mitchell argues, "this pattern is as inherent in our culture as it is in our biology . . . and we must remember there always *is* a father and it is the *idea* of him that Freud was commenting on" (*Woman's Estate*, 169–70). He *is* the history into which the (proto) subject is inserted. Mitchell contends: "He [Freud] examined the 'eternal' structures of patriarchy in what is for us their most essential particularity: the bourgeois, patriarchal family . . . The Oedipus complex is universal while the particular form used to redescribe it is specific" (*Psychoanalysis and Feminism*, 380–1; see Kaplan, 167).[12] The danger here for feminism is that the way psychoanalysis describes the structure of patriarchy may actually corroborate its oppressive order, in that the family in which human beings advene desire is posited as unchanging and unchangeable. That is, the oedipal situation becomes coterminous with the patriarchal family. Crucially, this conceptualization of the family – culturally constructed at the level of both the psychic and the social as the organizing principle of desire – is the mechanism that produces desire as transhistorical.

Psychoanalysis, then, does not theorize the way in which the family itself is socially determined, but rather attempts to explain the family in terms of itself, projecting the family of developed capitalist society onto all periods of history. This does not make psychoanalytic interpretation irrelevant to a materialist history of desire; it is the most compelling narrative of the psychic structuring of desire we possess and one that forestalls a purely functionalist understanding of its operations. Rather, psychoanalysis is relevant only insofar as it can be seen to undermine certain of its own assumptions – that is, when it can help to uncover the production of desire in patriarchal structures that are shifting and heterogeneous rather than static, monolithic, and universal.

While the "universalism" of psychoanalysis cannot be equated unproblematically with the universalizing of the liberal humanist tradition because the former disrupts rather than secures the coherent subject of the latter, it remains ironically true that in their dominant disciplinary formations psychoanalysis and history, despite their alleged antithesis, can be seen to rely upon strikingly similar notions of the patriarchal family. In Renaissance studies psychoanalysis is largely viewed as causally belated if not downright anachronistic, on the grounds that it erases temporal specificity by proposing a universal psychic scenario embedded in its foundational procedures and assumptions. History, in contrast, is typically understood as the common sense of our area of inquiry. Yet the history referred to is still what Jameson calls "the common garden-variety empirical history," that constitutes "bourgeois historiography" rather than "a genuine philosophy of history" (132; see also Cressy, 124). The result of this theoretical and ideological blind spot in the otherwise deservedly influential work of many social historians of the early modern era, such as Alan Macfarlane, David Cressy, and Keith Wrightson, is a prevailing tendency toward ahistoricism about desire and the nuclear family.

The ahistorical treatment of desire in early modern social history is especially apparent in the debate about the degree of continuity between Puritan ideals of love with those of prior and succeeding centuries.[13] It is now generally accepted that the conventional notion of the extended feudal family is misleading (Sharpe, 59–60). Even Lawrence Stone, much indicted for his insistence on change, does not deny a basic continuity: "most of the features of the modern family appeared before industrialization and among social groups unaffected by it and . . . even those exposed to it responded in different ways" (*The Family, Sex and Marriage*, 665).[14] This fact does not, however, obviate the need to account for the increasing pervasiveness of the ideology of nuclear familialism in early modern England, which required, produced, and interpellated female subjectivities of a *different* (though not necessarily "improved") order from those of preceding centuries (Newman, 20; Davies, 59). The permutations of the ideology of the family are significant for feminism because, as we have noted, that ideology constitutes a central structure in the psychic and social dimensions of women's oppression (Barrett, 251; Swindells and Jardine, 69). With the advent of capitalism, and the notion of private property, there is a new conception of the family as an independent economic unit within a market economy (Zaretsky, 32). The problem is that when social historians critique the naïve model of the shift from feudal clan to nuclear family and the now obsolete theory that Protestantism invariably offered conditions for women much improved from those of an allegedly benighted pre-Reformation Catholicism, they tend to collapse historical distinctions altogether and to relegate the ideological to the realm of ideas of a purely cognitive kind (Houlbrooke, 36). Further, the stress on the slow, almost imperceptible, evolution in the internal constitution of the household from the "extended" to the "nuclear" family is, as Eli Zaretsky points out, whether consciously or not, ideologically motivated: "Viewed in this way, the seeming inertia of the family has been in marked contrast to the continuous upheaval of political and economic history, a contrast that lends plausibility to the view that 'history' is the realm of politics and economics while the family is confined to 'nature'" (32).

In a recent essay, David Cressy indicts literary scholars for their allegedly naïve notions about the radical discontinuity in the history of the family attendant upon the advent of Protestantism, and especially their recourse to Lawrence Stone's *The Family, Sex and Marriage*:[15]

This is not just a professional squabble among historians, nor is it a technical dispute about sources. The disagreement goes to the heart of how we do history, about how we make sense of the past. Should we choose material to support pre-drawn conclusions, or should our argument be distilled from the sources? Is the past baffling and contradictory, or can we reduce it to patterns? . . . Nor are we dealing with a simple matter of taste, synchronic versus diachronic styles, or a predisposition toward watersheds and rifts rather than slow glacial flows. It comes down to evidence versus agenda. (130)

Clearly, it is important to move away from the reductive notion of history as straight-arrow teleology, but Cressy then returns us to an empiricist history which is essentially inscrutable, "baffling and contradictory." This is paradoxical since at the same time sources are seen as more or less transparent documents that will speak to the objective, "more cautious . . . more reliable" (130) historian who has laid all predrawn conclusions aside. Stone is not, of course, beyond the reach of criticism: he makes generalizations on the evidence of aristocratic families alone, for instance. For all that, what is at issue here is not simply the merits of Stone's book, but the politics of historiography. Cressy does not see that what constitutes "evidence" is itself the product of an "agenda" whether it be an explicitly political one concerned with struggle, conflict, and change, or merely a condition of bafflement.

Similarly, Keith Wrightson, whose book *English Society 1580–1680*, tries to account for both continuity and change, defines his conceptual hold upon the period in question as simply the product of "a *personal attempt* to bring together, to come to terms with and make sense of what has been revealed both of the nature of English society and of the course of social change within the century" (12, my emphasis). For Wrightson, change is never a matter of changes in state and economic structure; it is always a matter of "local diversity" (222):

Within the flexible structure of the neighbourhood there already flourished a cultural emphasis on the interests of the individual nuclear family which was a powerful enough incentive to override traditional social obligations where there was gain to be made. Such attitudes needed only the opportunity to express themselves more fully, and in the fiercely competitive climate of the late sixteenth and seventeenth centuries they found it. (223)

The family becomes naturalized, as does change itself – a "climate" which permits already existing conditions to flourish. Once again, the critique of Stone is instructive and indicative of a particular way of reading history:

[T]here is little reason to follow Professor Stone in regarding the rise of the companionate marriage as a new phenomenon of the later seventeenth and eighteenth centuries. It seems to have been already well established . . . It may well be that these are less evolutionary stages of familial progress, than the poles of an enduring continuum in marital relations in a society which accepted both the primacy of male authority and the ideal of marriage as a practical and emotional partnership. (Wrightson, 103–4)

In *Marriage and Love in England 1300–1840*, Alan Macfarlane (incidentally, Stone's best-known detractor) concedes like most other historians that while "the strengthening of the husband–wife bond is part of . . . emotional and economic nucleation" (174), which is regarded as one of the preconditions of modernity, and a distinctive feature of western families – "it is not the pivot of social structure in the majority of societies" (174) – he proceeds to go back and forth across centuries and genres to show that things were always the same from Anglo-Saxon England to the nineteenth century:

As far back as we can easily go, there is evidence of the same insistence. If we leap back to the early thirteenth century we find in the encyclopedia by Bartholomaeus Anglicus a similar emphasis on love, "fellowship", affection, consideration . . . [T]he revolution to conjugality and companionate marriage, which is both unusual and so influential, had occurred at least by the time of Chaucer in England, if not long before. (183)

In fact "continuity" – a perfectly valid if not entirely accurate postulate – has been erased by the complete collapse of historical difference. It would undoubtedly be futile to argue that human beings have not felt genuine emotional intimacy and overwhelming desire through the ages, but the form, figure, and meaning of these phenomena are historically specific. Macfarlane's text is symptomatic of a prevailing tendency toward ahistoricism among early modern social historians about the social construction of desire institutionalized as marriage and the nuclear family. He devotes a chapter on romantic love almost entirely to literary "evidence." The argument for the ubiquity of a uniform romantic love is not adequately supported by the great list of literary quotations Macfarlane offers by way of historical verification. I am not arguing here that literary texts are irrelevant to history: my own text takes Shakespeare's play as a cultural document of a particular historical circumstance. But I find it impossible to agree with Macfarlane that *Romeo and Juliet* figures as the acme of and the evidence for timeless love:

> The passion of love in its myriad manifestations is brought into conflict with a thousand obstacles, and the resolution of these difficulties keeps audiences in the past and today in a state of suspense and enchantment . . . reaching exquisite perfection in *Romeo and Juliet*. (184)

Romantic love is here completely divorced from social considerations so that it becomes a transhistorical "emotion." In short, desire is placed resolutely outside history; untouched by temporal and other differences.[16]

Paradoxically, then, historians arrive at a view of the family which bears an uncanny resemblance to its situation in psychoanalysis. The family, it turns out, is for social historians, as much as it is for a psychoanalytic theorist like Juliet Mitchell, "a *relatively* constant unit in relation to the entire course of social history. As such, it has a certain autonomy and inflexibility, whatever the stage of economic development of the society as a whole" (*Woman's Estate*, 159).[17] The point here is not that such an assertion, whether enunciated by psychoanalytic critics or social historians, is ludicrously retrograde; it is rather that both psychoanalysis and history are epistemological configurations whose ostensible antipathy has obscured their shared participation in the cultural processes whereby the family is peculiarly insulated from historical change, and thus desire, produced within the family and circulated among families, is excluded from the process of historicization.

A final example from the debate about Stone will perhaps make clear why, despite its shortcomings, the overall conception of his book remains useful. For Stone, the modern family of capitalist development is presented as a more significant site of sexual and emotional satisfaction than its early modern precursor. He has been attacked for the proposition that there could have been little emotional investment in families in former times because of arranged marriages and high rates of infant mortality; people surely loved one another and grieved for one another in the past as now. However, when social historians critical of Stone take up this point, they use this issue as a way of asserting the universality of emotional investment in family life. That "affection, co-operation and mutual give-and-take" may have existed in early modern domestic arrangements, or even "passionate attachment" (Sharpe, 69, 62) is not, therefore, identical with the *ideology* through which these relations are constituted. The conceptual tools of social historians simply do not allow for a distinction between sexual passions and the ideology of romantic love with which we are concerned. As a result, they are blind to the distinct, historically mutable *material effects* of ideology. Of course, neither does Stone have a theory of ideology, and so it is only a Marxist-feminist reading of Stone that can account for social change in the social institutions which structure and regulate human intimacy.

Desire and the Postmodern Present

Renaissance literary studies, in contrast to social history, has been less impervious to postmodern interrogations of history as an epistemological configuration – that is, the discursive practices, rhetorical devices, and narrative strategies through which historical knowledge is constituted (see Novick, 545–6).[18] Postmodern interrogations of history are diametrically opposed to the verities of traditional historiography, especially the belief that "historical facts are prior to and independent of interpretation" (Novick, 2). This cognitive revolution may be characterized as the recognition that history is an epistemological category, even an anachronism relying upon causality and teleology and the exclusion of "marginal" populations, and that history no longer functions as a simple container for immutable essences with their superficial temporal and cultural variations.[19] As Alice Jardine has pointed out, "even history – that most encompassing of master narratives, the one to which we in the West have always been able to turn as a last resort – becomes problematic in and of itself (it becomes historicizable) and turns back upon itself" (81). Significantly, the postmodern crisis of history can be seen in Renaissance studies in its engagement with psychoanalysis. I will offer two symptomatic and important examples of this phenomenon rather than an exhaustive survey of it.

In *Fashioning Femininity*, Karen Newman argues that the details of English witchcraft practice may be "mere incidentals" for social historians, but for her they "adumbrate a peculiar narrative of motherhood and the unconscious" (58). Further, she defends the use of pychoanalysis, which "need not inevitably make ahistorical claims about human development that preclude historical analysis" (62), on the Derridean grounds that a text's context is limitless, there is no ground, no center: "there are only contexts" (65). Nonetheless, Newman's attempt to make psychoanalysis and history compatible rests on deconstructive undecidability: "the object of sexuality is socially and ideologically produced in a given culture," the "unfixed," and "denaturalized" "precarious" result of historical evolution (63). While this remains a sophisticated interrogation of the interrelation between the two categories, it does not explain why denaturalizing and unfixing in and of themselves help us historicize. For instance the trajectory of women in patriarchal history, although not inevitable, presents a compulsively repetitive narrative rather than an undecidable one. The endless unfixings Newman proposes, while they certainly free her compelling readings from the limitations of traditional historical methods as well as from essentially allegorical, mechanical applications of psychoanalysis to the literary text, obscure the determinate positions of the oppressed. Newman's emphasis is not the material oppression of women, but the profoundly post-structuralist "threat posed through representation" dangerously unmoored from material conditions (69). Crucial though this strategy is, it remains difficult to see how Newman's use of psychoanalysis, apart from the mere assertion of historicism, differs substantially from those she critiques.

Stephen Greenblatt's brilliant and pathbreaking 1986 essay, "Psychoanalysis and Renaissance culture," argues for a complex rather than a categorical disjunction between the early modern period and the post-psychoanalytic moment. He suggests we can discern in the early modern era the conditions which gave rise to the development of psychoanalysis.[20] That is, the Renaissance helped "fashion the historical mode of selfhood that psychoanalysis has tried to universalize into the very form of the human condition" (216). For Greenblatt, "[p]sychoanalysis is . . . less the privileged explanatory key than the distant and distorted consequence of this cultural nexus" (216). Renaissance subjectivity, then becomes "more an historical condition that enables the development of psychoanalysis than a psychic condition that psychoanalysis itself can adequately explain" (221).

What is at stake in Greenblatt's critique, however, is not psychoanalysis itself, which it soon becomes clear he finds wholly inadequate for a truly historical project – "the universalist claims of psychoanalysis are unruffled by the indifference of the past to its categories" (215) – but rather the postmodern crisis of history in which there is no "solid and single truth, or (in more subtle versions) interesting variants on the central and irreducible universal narrative, the timeless master myth" (217). There are only *"histories,* – multiple, complex, refractory stories" (217). While this position does threaten the coherence of liberal, empiricist history, and while these multiple histories do not claim to be value-neutral, Greenblatt's invocation of multiplicity is, nonetheless, almost identical with the value-neutral relativism he eschews. His position is a post-structuralist one, of undecidable (undecided) political and logical investment: "the intimations of an obscure link between . . . distant events and the way we are" (217). History again subsumes psychoanalysis, and the account of our desires, "the way we are," becomes almost mysteriously unknowable.

The demise of history as *grand récit,* replaced by a sophisticated if diffuse understanding of "a network of lived and narrated stories, practices, strategies, representations, fantasies, negotiations, and exchanges that, along with the surviving aural, tactile, and visual traces, fashion our experience of the past, of others, and of ourselves" (218) may finally share the ideological effects of the liberal model it purports to replace.[21] In its postmodern and new historicist renovation, history has more texture, "complexity" and aesthetic appeal, but it does not offer a conceptual frame possessed of expanded powers of explanation. Specifically, it evades the motivating dynamic of historical contestation, the operations whereby all representations are not equal; some are repressed and deleted beyond any resuscitation or reinstatement that might be effected by new historicist methods.[22]

In contrast, a materialist history of desire, in this case one which takes *Romeo and Juliet* as its literary object, entails an insistence on the holistic claims of Marxist historical methods, which (very often) collide head on with the micro-analyses of essentialist social historians. Indeed, an insistence on certain global conceptual categories distinguishes materialist analysis from a local, purely textual one. For historical materialism is not about amassing historical detail; it is about history as structured material conflict.

The play produces one version of desire as paramount among the range of those it negotiates, and in doing so participates in the cultural production of desire required by the rise of absolutism, the centralization of the state, and the advent of capitalism. These developments, while not linear and continuous historical developments, constitute the advent of modernity, and it is surely only the burden of traditional critical practice that has contrived to place them as either remote from or irrelevant to the textual details of Renaissance drama (see Anderson, *Lineages*, 8–10). The hegemonic ideology of romantic love is crucially related to some of the definitive conditions of nascent modernity: the construction within the domestic sphere of the realm of the personal, an increased emphasis on the nucleated unit rather than the extended clan, the reinforcement of patriarchy in the household and in the absolutist state, and the advent of absolute private property in land (see Anderson, *Lineages*, 25–6).[23] The point here is not to concentrate on the conjunctural level (that is, to draw extensive analogies between the text and the broad shift from one form of economic organization to another) but on the prior conceptual one (antecedent in the mediation between chains of intelligibilities). That is, *Romeo and Juliet* does not exemplify the actual, empirical, social circumstances of its production, but rather participates and intervenes in the ideological/historical conditions of its own making.

Patriarchal Law and the Centralization of the State

The move from the family allegiances associated with feudalism to those identified with centralization of the state constitutes the overarching narrative of *Romeo and Juliet*. That is, the *shifting configurations* of patriarchal law and the changing formations of desire which attend it comprise the structure and substance of Shakespeare's text.[24] In this sense, the play articulates a crisis in patriarchy itself – specifically the transference of power from the feuding fathers to the Prince so that sexual desire in the form presented here produces the required subjectivities and harnesses them for the state above all other possible levels of allegiance. Desire needs to be refigured in order to manage the contradiction produced by the way the ideology of absolutism employed familial rhetoric in order to maintain feudal domination and exploitation despite the advent of a commodity economy (see Anderson, *Lineages*, 19).[25] As a result, the mode of desire disapproved of in the old order becomes valorized in the new one. However, that the ideological project of *Romeo and Juliet* is now completely coincident with the dominant ideology of desire does not mean that the play circulates only one discourse of desire. Rather, multiple and contradictory discourses of the desire are negotiated in the isolation and idealization of romantic heterosexual love.

That desire seems malleable, something that can be reordered, is apparent in Mercutio's Queen Mab speech, which charts the various courses a disembodied libido can take, from the sexual desires of women – kisses of ladies to the unseemly lust of maids – to the greed and blood-lust of men:

> And in this state she gallops night by night
> Through lovers' brains, and then they dream of love;
> O'er courtiers' knees that dream on cur'sies straight
> O'er lawyers' fingers, who straight dream on fees;
> O'er ladies' lips, who straight on blisters dream,
> Which oft the angry Mab with kisses plagues,
> Because their breath with sweetmeats tainted are . . .
> Sometime she driveth o'er a soldier's neck,
> And then dreams he of cutting foreign throats,
> Of breaches, ambuscadoes, Spanish blades . . .
> This is the hag, when maids lie on their backs,
> That presses them and makes them first to bear,
> Making them women of good carriage
>
> (I. iv. 70–94)

Although a force penetrating the unconscious of the dreamer from outside, desire is already socially scripted here (ladies and maids do not dream of cutting soldiers throats); it is not "free." (There is no desire hovering in some metaphysical space prior to its social production.) Desire is simultaneously controlled and aberrant, chaotic – its objective is either death or reproduction: "For this drivelling love is like a great natural that runs lolling up and down to hide his bauble in a hole" (II. iv. 91–3). In Mercutio's comic teleology, desire is directed, driven, and yet indiscriminate about its sexual object – a "drive" in the psychoanalytic sense.

That it is Mercutio who articulates the plasticity of desire is particularly significant.[26] His cynicism, as well as his sexual predilection for men and his kinship with the Prince rather than the warring feudal houses, enables him to articulate the social construction of desire in which his companions are too fully invested. No maidens weep for Mercutio when he is killed. Rather, Escalus and Romeo are the characters who bear the loss of the master of the phallic pun. When Escalus comments on the lovers' tragedy, he also refers to his private grief for "a brace of kinsmen," of whom Mercutio is the one we know by name (V. iii. 295). As absolutist monarch,

Escalus seems to retain homoeroticism among his kin group. If this notion seems implausible to us, it is probably because, as Bruce Smith points out, we think of social sites of sexual experience as exclusively private and of sexuality in terms of "acts" rather than as relational dynamics:

> For us, the most significant loci of sexuality are private life and the family. It was during the sixteenth and seventeenth centuries that sexuality first came to be seen as a private concern, but sexuality was located even more solidly within social institutions that strike us today as remote or inappropriate. (21)

The male power structure in general was indeed itself a force which generated male homoerotic desire, and with the rise of absolutism "the explicit disparities in power that animated homosexual desire in early modern England" (Smith, 23) would have been focused with increasing intensity on the figure of the monarch himself. It is the Prince who monopolizes male bonding, aggression, and homoerotic desire.[27]

Yet Escalus also attempts to direct the multiple possible modes of desire in socially appropriate, explicitly heterosexual ways. Indeed, in a number of important respects it is Prince Escalus who becomes the play's pivotal figure rather than the tragic couple. Shakespeare imposes the ordering principle embodied in Escalus on Brooke's rambling structure at the play's opening, closing, and center so that the strong literary design is coincident with the authority he wields in turbulent Verona (see Gibbons, 39). In addition, in Shakespeare's symbolic redistribution of the city's property, Escalus is accorded a castle in Freetown, which belongs to Capulet in Brooke and Painter, and to which he summons Montague and Capulet from their more humble merchants' homes after the first disturbance of the peace (see Gibbons, 87).

More importantly, Escalus intervenes in the feud with absolute power of life and death. Even that intervention, however, is not immediately effective because he must struggle to become the preeminent patriarchal power in Verona. The Law of the Father in the psychoanalytic framework is constituted by precisely the power of intervention – that which disrupts in the dyad of mother and child, as the symbolic representative of culture. Although Escalus is essentially intervening between fathers, he nonetheless takes the place of the father in relation to the infantile feuding, feudal fathers who resist the exogamous relationship between their offspring, objecting to their quarrel as profane, bestial, and "cankered" (I. i. 82–95). As Coppélia Kahn points out, Prince Escalus "embodies the law," and in relation to him it is "Montague and Capulet who are childishly refractory" (172):

> Rebellious subjects, enemies to peace,
> Profaners of this neighbour-stained steel –
> Will they not hear? What ho! You men, you beasts!
> That quench the fire of your pernicious rage
> With purple fountains issuing from your veins,
> On pain of torture from those bloody hands
> Throw your mistempered weapons to the ground
> And hear the sentence of your moved prince.
>
> (I. i. 81–8)

Escalus strives to control the flow of blood, a metonym of lineage, class, and succession – the very essence of the patriarchal imperative. In so doing, the dangers of consanguinity are displaced onto the feuding feudal family:

> Two households, both alike in dignity,
> In fair Verona, where we lay our scene,
> From ancient grudge break to new mutiny,
> Where civil blood makes civil hands unclean.
> From forth the fatal loins of these two foes
> A pair of star-cross'd lovers take their life.
>
> (Prologue, 1–6)

In this passage, the symmetry between the houses suggests an ominous familial resemblance. The ancient blood they share is the bloodshed of enmity. They are star-crossed by a common inheritance – the brutal engagement that has in enmity mangled and enmeshed the blood and loins of their houses so that, as Kay Stockholder has argued, their relationship verges precariously on the incestuous:

The image of "fatal loins" suggests a kind of copulation in hatred between the feuding families . . . It suggests that they die not because they are children of warring families, but rather that their feuding parents are the circumstances of their meeting, their loving, and their death. The same magnetism that brings the two families together in order to fight also brings the two young people together in order to love and die. (30)[28]

Thus for Stockholder the lovers' marriage merely continues the feud. Although this is certainly the case in Bandello's prior version of the story where Romeo and Juliet's love ignited a well-nigh extinct enmity, it is not the case in Shakespeare where the lovers mark the end of incest and the beginning of exogamy, the emergent ideology of the family. We see this, for example, in Juliet's ironic articulation of the transfer of her desire from kin to foe upon Tybalt's death: "To wreak the love I bore my cousin / Upon his body that hath slaughtered him!" (III. v. 101–2). The Prince's prohibition against the feud is, then, synonymous with a prohibition against endogamy – "the sentence of your moved prince" (I. i. 88) – and it is a prohibition with which Romeo and Juliet almost instinctively comply.[29]

In contrast to the civil and civilizing intervention of the Prince, the atrophied, macerated power of the belligerent secular fathers is rendered in comic fashion in the brawl scene of Act I, where they appear in ridiculous *déshabillé*:

(*Enter old Capulet in his gown, and his Wife.*)
Capulet: What noise is this? Give me my long sword ho!
Lady Capulet: A crutch, a crutch! Why call you for a sword?
Capulet: My sword, I say! Old Montague is come,
                    And flourishes his blade in spite of me.
(*Enter old Montague and his Wife.*)
Montague: Thou villain Capulet! – Hold me not; let me go.
Lady Montague: Thou shalt not stir one foot to seek a foe.
                                        (I. i. 75–80)

It is the women here who deflate the exaggerated phallic proportions of their husbands, whose long swords refer us back to Sampson and Gregory's "comic" meditations on erection and rape that began the affray. Lady Montague's command prefaces the Prince's admonition that the battle end on pain of death. In her mouth the injunction is an instance of comic inversion of authority, and it serves both to align her with the will of the Prince, as opposed to the will of her husband, and to show that her husband cannot rule even his own wife.

Old Capulet's power is equally diminished. While well able to rail at his daughter he cannot control the precocious Tybalt, whose libido is violently unleashed upon the world:

        The fiery Tybalt, with his sword prepar'd;
        Which, as he breath'd defiance to my ears,

> He swung about his head cutting the winds,
> Who, nothing hurt withal, hissed him in scorn.
>
> (I. i. 109–12)

There is a marked contrast here with the manageable masculinity of Romeo, with whom Tybalt seeks mortal engagement at the Capulet festivities, who is "so secret and so close, / So far from sounding" (I. i. 149–50). Unlike Romeo, Tybalt refuses to take his proper place in the hierarchy of male authority:

> *Capulet*:   He shall be endured.
> What, goodman boy? I say he shall. Go to!
> Am I the master here, or you? Go to!
> You'll not endure him! God shall mend my soul,
> You'll make a mutiny among my guests!
> You will set cock-a-hoop! You'll be the man!
>
> (I. v. 76–81)

Capulet derides Tybalt with the diminutives "saucy boy" and "princox," which depredate Tybalt's phallic pretensions to "set cock-a-hoop" (I. v. 81–6). The inappropriate phallic competition here is not resolved but, like Freud's account of the child's submission to the Law of the Father, is deferred with a view to later satisfaction:

> Patience perforce with willful choler meeting
> Makes my flesh tremble in their different greeting.
> I will withdraw, but this intrusion shall,
> Now seeming sweet, convert to bitt'rest gall.
>
> (I. v. 89–92)

Tybalt's trembling flesh resembles the agitated state of *coitus interruptus* in the language of his withdrawal and the visitors' intrusion; his erotic object is a highly sexualized violence.

Capulet's intervention clearly lacks decisive power. Nonetheless, no matter how diminished their authority the presence of the fathers of both Church and household is what threatens the power of the Prince. The benign and dangerously ineffectual Friar Lawrence must become abject before Escalus's castrating power, finally submitting himself "Unto the rigour of severest law" (V. iii. 269) in order that Prince Escalus appropriate the castrating capacity which constitutes the Law of the Father.

The consolidation of Escalus's power is evident in the play's conclusion when the warring fathers make a belated public solemnization of the marriage contract:

Capulet: O brother Montague, give me thy hand.
This is my daughter's jointure, for no more
Can I demand.

(V. iii. 296–8)

The end of enmity is contingent upon the feuding fathers' submission to the Prince:

Prince: Capulet! Montague!
See what a scourge is laid upon your hate,
That heaven finds means to kill your joys with love.
And I for winking at your discords too,
Have lost a brace of kinsmen. All are punish'd.

(V. iii. 291–5)

The result of this shift in power is "glooming peace" and its price has been the sacrifice of the fathers' children (V. iii. 305).

A crucial dimension of Escalus's appropriation of the power of the secular and religious fathers, as we noted at the outset, is the control over the narrative of the love tragedy. It is Romeo's letter to his father that becomes, amid a series of recapitulations of the play's tragic matter, the version of events authorized by the Prince for further dissemination:

Balthasar: I brought my master news of Juliet's death;
And then in post he came from Mantua
To this same place, to this same monument.
This letter he early bid me give his father,
And threat'ned me with death, going in the vault,
If I departed not and left him there.
Prince: Give me the letter. I will look on it . . .
This letter doth make good the friar's words,
The course of love, the tidings of her death . . .

(V. iii. 272–87ff)

This missive, like the Friar's letter to Romeo, does not reach its intended destination, but instead is confiscated by the Prince who symbolically absorbs the power of Romeo's father – "I will look on it" – even though the mourning Montague, its intended recipient, is himself fully available to peruse it. In taking the role of coordinator and interpreter of the various renditions of the tragic events in the play's coda (the Friar's, Balthasar's), the Prince consolidates his power over the errant feudal forces that have previously sought to dissipate it. This monopoly on interpretation is appropriate given Romeo's earlier alignment with the Prince's peace, under whose auspices he made the fatal intervention that cost Mercutio his life, "the Prince expressly hath/Forbid this bandying in Verona streets" (III. i. 88–9). What the Prince expropriates in taking up Romeo's letter is his legacy to the world. The letter serves as a symbolic substitute for the "name" he would have passed on to posterity had he survived to produce progeny with Juliet. In this sense, his letter resonates with the play's earlier concern with the politics of naming (II. iv. 39–40). The issue of Romeo's name stands in direct relation to his tragic struggle to articulate an identity distinct from the feudal one he wished to revoke. It is this version of identity – defined in terms of interiority and individual autonomy – and desire, disarticulated from the animosities of the feud (Romeo but not a Montague, so to speak), that the play unambiguously validates. For it is the identity required by what the tragic couple represent, namely, the tragic inauguration of a romantic love validated by marriage.

Institutionalizing "Unconstrained" Love: The Rise of the Nuclear Family

As I have argued, *Romeo and Juliet* makes its cultural intervention at a moment when the ideology of love and marriage and the organization of desire required to sustain it is undergoing change. In its articulation by Protestant (mainly Puritan) churchmen, the paradigm of marriage was profoundly imbued with idealism, stressing less the evils of voracious female sexuality, as earlier writings had done, and more the benefits of pliant femininity (see Newman, 27). The production of female desire is the mechanism whereby female subjectivities were recruited to changing understandings of marriage and society. The Puritan doctrine of marriage requires nothing less than that women are endowed with desiring subjectivity, which can then be actively solicited and controlled by the social order. The crude sexual and economic exchange of enforced marriage is displaced by the concept of freely circulating love (especially freedom of choice about one's marriage partner) and wealth. Thus, despite the contradictions entailed in the Protestant articulation of domestic harmony, namely, the superiority of the husband versus the "equality" of his wife who is both helpmate and subject, and the endeavor to bolster the often competing power of *both* husbands and fathers, romantic marriage is inscribed with a displaced utopianism. At the ideological level at least, buttressed by lyric and aesthetic convention, marriage has not yet disintegrated into the more mundane bourgeois monogamy described by Kristeva as "the banal, humdrum, lackluster lassitude of a tired and cynical collusion: that is the normal marriage" (217).

In *Romeo and Juliet*, we see the idealization of desire situated within lyrical and tragic aesthetic conventions which distance the play from the practical tone of the marriage treatises whose ideological project it shares. While the lovers are thwarted by external forces, their frustration is of an entirely different order from that of Romeo's unrequited love for Rosaline. Romeo and Juliet's love at least entails physical consummation after a very brief courtship in which Juliet has been surprisingly forthright about her desires:

> but farewell, compliment!
> Dost thou love me? I know thou wilt say "Ay,"
> And I will take thy word; yet, if thou swear'st,
> Thou mayest prove false: at lovers' perjuries
> They say, Jove laughs. O gentle Romeo,
> If thou dost love, pronounce it faithfully.
> Or, if thou thinkest I am too quickly won,
> I'll frown and be perverse, and say thee nay,
> So thou wilt woo, but else not for the world.
> In truth, fair Montague, I am too fond,
> And therefore thou mayest think my behaviour light,
> But trust me, gentleman, I'll prove more true
> Than those that have [more] coying to be strange.
> (II. ii. 89–101)

While there are traces of Catholic reticence about sexual desire in the late sixteenth-century drama,[30] in *Romeo and Juliet*, the symbolic systems of Catholicism – pilgrimage, the palmer's kiss, veneration of saints, and the sacrament of confession – are displaced onto the rites of specifically sexual love. In the above passage, Juliet refuses to engage further in these elaborate, ritualized negotiations and exchanges of erotic power that constitute courtship. This is attributable to the fact that the play is not about power within the couple – this is completely idealized – but about the power relation between the amorous couple and the outside world. The lovers' free choice of each other seems to dissolve the power relation between them and to absolve them of the necessity to defer to any authority other than their own. Indeed, it is the idealization of the couple's love that aligns *Romeo and Juliet* with comedy and repeatedly suggests, despite forebodings to the contrary, the possibility of a happy conclusion.

In Act I, scene ii, where the initial desires of both lovers are presented, the perimeters of his daughter's desire are laid out by Capulet:

> But woo her, gentle Paris, get her heart,
> My will to her consent is but a part;
> And she agreed, within her scope of choice
> Lies my consent and fair according voice.
>   (I. ii. 16–19)

Capulet is woefully unaware of what is required to get his daughter's heart, or of the power differential that constitutes the distance between his will and the troublesome issue of female consent. The passion of romantic love requires an inexplicable and mutual abandonment of "mastery." It is mutuality, of course, that signals the crucial difference between Romeo's infatuation with Rosaline and his love for Juliet: "Now Romeo is beloved and loves again, / Alike bewitched by the charm of looks" (II, Prologue, 5–6). Critics have remarked upon the occult connotations of "bewitched," but bewitched also implies enchantment as a psychological state, an erotically charged ideological interpellation. Juliet has no choice about the depth to which she will "endart" her gaze on Romeo, because the condition of love she experiences is far in excess of either her own will or that of her father. The mutuality of mirrored passion fosters the notion that one's authentic identity is revealed in romantic love.

It is important to emphasize the degree to which this freedom of choice in marriage is linked to economic considerations, especially the oxymoronic notion of "free exchange." Unconstrained choice about one's marriage partner relies to some degree on the ideological separation of psychic and monetary economies. Ideally, both parents and child will agree

on a match, but what is at stake here is not so much the right of liberty
in love, as an endeavor to prevent parents marrying off their children
for financial gain, a phenomenon which became more marked with the
bourgeoisification of the aristocracy. George Whetstone writes:

> I cry out upon forcement in Marriage, as the extremest bondage that
> is . . . the father thinks he hath a happy purchase, if he get a rich young ward
> to match with his daughter: but God he knows, and the unfortunate couple
> often feel that he buyeth sorrow to his child, slander to himself and per-
> chance the ruin of an ancient gentleman's house by the riot of the son in law
> not loving his wife. (Cited in Macfarlane, *Marriage and Love*, 134)

The situation here is addressed in explicitly economic terms. Similarly, the
Tell-Trothes New-Yeares Gift (1595) complained, "when as parents do by
compulsion couple two bodies, neither respecting the joining of their
hearts, nor having any care of the continuance of their welfare, but more
regarding the linking of wealth and money together, than love with
honesty" (*Marriage and Love*, 134–5). While this concern may not be
unique to this period, it is newly emphasized. Indeed, Peter Laslett has
argued that it is precisely as a result of "choice and deliberation" in
marriage – evident in the large gap between reproductive age and age of
marriage and a high rate of non-marriage – that permits the development
of capitalism in the West ("The European family," 236).

Lady Capulet's statement that "Thou hast a careful father, child" –
suggests that he is not only solicitous but perhaps penurious, and in the
scene where he tries to coerce Juliet's consent to the match with Paris, he
does it by negating female power – silencing all the women around him,
"Speak not, reply not, do not answer me!" (III. v. 106, 163). The Nurse
rebels, "May not one speak," "I speak no treason," while Lady Capulet, the
obedient wife, vows "I'll not speak a word" (III. v, 173, 172, 202). Only
after such pressure upon her attempted intervention, in a gesture more
pragmatic than immoral, does the Nurse advise her charge to comply with
the paternal order. Despite his initial uncertainty – "to soon marr'd are
those so early made?" (I. ii. 13) – Capulet's concern with financial gain and
social status is thoroughly apparent; it is even more so in Quarto 1 where
the line about the statues at the end of the play reads "no figure shall at
such price be set." As Michael Mooney has observed, the sense is then one
of cost rather than value (131). The warring feudal families here become an

amalgam of warring nobility and rising bourgeois merchants engaged in economic competition, both of which offered some threat to absolutism (Anderson, *Lineages*, 19–22). Military antagonism in which fixed quantities of ground are won or lost is replaced by a more benign economic engagement (though of course, historically, it proved the downfall of absolutism) wherein rival parties may both expand and prosper "because the production manufactured commodities is inherently unlimited" (*Lineages*, 31).

In contrast to the formal settlement arrived at in Capulet's negotiations with Paris, in the dealings of the lovers, the Nurse is the unruly woman, the comic agent of their *ad hoc* marriage arrangements. Her disorderly transactions are reminiscent of the illicit exchanges of the brothel. Hence, Mercutio calls out, "A bawd! A bawd! A bawd!" (II. iv. 130):

Romeo: Here's for thy pains.
Nurse: No truly, sir; not a penny.
Romeo: Go to, I say you shall.
                (II. iv. 182–4)

Significantly, the financial power here is in the hands of Romeo, not the bride's father, as Romeo recognized at the moment he discovered Juliet's identity: "O dear account! My life is my foe's debt" (I. v. 118); "As that vast shore [wash'd] with the farthest sea, / I should adventure for such merchandise" (II. ii. 83–4). That is, his "free" choice is bolstered by economic independence. Just before their marriage, Juliet too refers to her dowry:

> They are but beggars that can count their worth,
> But my true love is grown to such excess
> I cannot sum up sum of half my wealth.
>   (II. v. 32–4)

That her "wealth" consists of love rather than property exemplifies the shift here, and again it is she not her father who controls it. Financial metaphors reconfigure patriarchal economic transactions. Thus, the reordering of desire is attendant on the economic transformations sketched above – though of course in the play these transformations are metaphoric rather than literal – and the ideology of romantic love works to obscure them. We know, for instance, that there was considerable struggle over financial matters between husbands and wives. William Gouge's *Of Domesticall*

Duties (1622) defensively seeks to placate those women whose remonstrance he endured after preaching at St Paul's that women should defer to their husbands in the matter of the wives' personal property: "This just apologie I have been forced to make, that I might not ever be judged (as some have censured me) an hater of women" (3–4).

Wayward Female Desire

There is, then, in *Romeo and Juliet*, a production of a specific form of female desire, benign and unthreatening, easily recruited to emergent absolutism and nascent capitalism. Whereas in the figure of Mercutio there is an alternative to the kind of heterosexual masculine desire that Romeo comes to represent by the end of the play, there appears to be no radically alternative regime of female sexuality to that represented by Juliet. However, this is not quite the case. For in Act I, scene iii there is a production of a highly sexualized, ribald female desire that parallels the "rough love" of male homoeroticism that immediately follows in the next scene in the exchanges of the "lusty gentlemen" Benvolio, Romeo, and Mercutio (I. iv. 25, 112). The purpose of this scene is to inform Juliet of the marriage negotiations between Capulet and the County Paris, but what emerges is a women's scene, which disrupts the patriarchal project by presenting maternal eroticism, child sexuality, and female bawdy. The scene is freighted with multiple erotic possibilities, and in particular it is the displaced nature of maternality that produces a form of eroticism neither generated nor contained by the patriarchal order, feudal or otherwise.

In the very opening lines of the scene, Lady Capulet makes formal demand to the Nurse for "my daughter" (I. iii. i). The Nurse's summons in itself produces a range of female erotic possibilities:

> Now, by my maidenhead at twelve year old,
> I bade her come. What, lamb! What, lady-bird!
> God forbid! Where's this girl? What Juliet!
> (I. iii. 3–5)

The Nurse's comic invocation of her long-departed maidenhead suggests a connection between her own "grotesque" body, with its four teeth and over-sucked dugs (grotesque insofar as it insists on its excess of the contained limits of the "classical" body) and the maidenhead of "this girl," Juliet, who is the object of affections which exceed the class-demarcated bounds of maternal propriety: "lamb!"; "lady-bird!" (I. iii. 3–4). The point here, of course, is not to suggest that Juliet is the victim of the Nurse's improper sexual conduct, but rather that the business of nursing is itself sexual in ways that are difficult to grasp because nursing is now almost completely desexualized. It is interesting to compare the mutual pleasure of "giving suck," where the woman actively provides oral gratification to the infant she nurtures with the pleasures of fellatio. Almost all the sexual dimensions of sucking have now been transferred to the latter practice and therefore onto the male organ.

The Nurse offers a sensual recollection of Juliet's weaning:

> And she was wean'd – I never shall forget it –
> Of all the days of the year upon that day;
> For I had then laid wormwood to my dug,
> Sitting in the sun under the dove house wall.
> My lord and you were then at Mantua –
> Nay, I do bear a brain – but, as I said,
> When it did it taste the wormwood on the nipple
> Of my dug, and felt it bitter, pretty fool,
> To see it teachy, and fall out wi' th' dug!
>
>   (I. iii. 24–32)

The fact that the Nurse is a comic figure has all too often obscured the fact that she bears events as indelible maternal memory: "I never shall forget"; "I do bear a brain." Juliet is weaned by the Nurse while her parents are away, a process which seems to mark her as an initiate of sexual knowledge:

> For then she could stand high-lone; nay, by th' rood,
> She could have run and waddled all about;
> For even the day before, she broke her brow,
> And then my husband – God be with his soul!
> 'A was a merry man – took up the child.
> "Yea," quoth he, "dost thou fall upon thy face?
> Thou wilt fall backward when thou hast more wit,
> Wilt thou not, Jule?" and, by my holidam,
> The pretty wretch left crying and said "Ay."
>
>   (I. iii. 36–44)

The Nurse extends the sexualization of this recollection by adding to the description of Juliet a phallic "bump as big as a young cockerel's stone," that recalls the violence of heterosexual relations, and is reminiscent of her later remark that "bigger; women grow by men" (I. iii. 53, 95). In contrast, it is Lady Capulet who invokes the romantic imagery of "This precious book of love" (I. iii. 87), which dominates the rest of the play.

This scene, then, represents in palimpsest, female sensuality, maternity, and eroticism which, while they are clearly subordinated to patriarchal rule in the feudal order have become virtually unintelligible, undiscernible, in our own.

Genre and Ideology in the Tragic Ending

The post-coital satisfaction of Romeo and Juliet as autonomous conjugal unit is short-lived and remarkably clandestine. Tragic events never allow time to fulfill the Friar's hopes of making the marriage public: "To blaze your marriage, reconcile your friends" (III. iii. 151–4). Bruce Smith argues "Mercutio may die, but only bad timing keeps *Romeo and Juliet* from reaching the comic conclusion of married love" (64). In this he points to the crucial distinction between the demise of the erotic mode represented by Mercutio and that represented by the lovers.

Had it not been aimed at sexual access rather than escape with Juliet, Romeo's rope-ladder scheme (Gibbons, 92) might have avoided the tragic conclusion. In fact, the legitimate secrecy, so to speak, of "privacy" is the order in which such a love as that of Romeo and Juliet would thrive.[31] The marriage of Romeo and Juliet could, after all, have provided the diplomatic solution to the feud; this pragmatic solution is opposed by the fathers so that the apparently antithetical ideal of romantic love as autonomous and inherently resistant to all social constraints can be incorporated into the diplomatic solution.[32] In fact, Romeo and Juliet's love, while it offers resistance to their feudal households is perfectly compatible with the interests of society as a whole. Thus, the utopian, dangerous, and paradoxical notion of a law that ratifies (inherently transgressive) passion, becomes the desideratum of early modern marriage (see Kristeva, 210).

The lovers' desire as both transgressive and a new orthodoxy indicates the dislocation and relocation of authority that I have argued occurs by the end of the play. Yet, very clearly, the play is not didactic. As Frank Kermode puts it, albeit in the rhetoric of authorial intent,

[W]e should beware of supposing that Shakespeare's sympathies lay strongly in this or that direction; that he was on the Friar's side when he uttered the conventional condemnation of the lovers in a story which must always have thrived on their attractiveness; or, on the other hand, that he was committed to this surreptitious but virtuous passion as in itself of the highest value. (Evans et al., 1057)

What is at stake is not simply an endorsement of the desire of the lovers or the control of the fathers; it is whether the play is an argument for absolutism, whether it approves the government of the crown above all others. This does not, however, mean that fathers are now without authority (see Stone, *The Family, Sex and Marriage*, ch. 5). Rather, *Romeo and Juliet* addresses some of the contradictions in post-Reformation patriarchy where there is an endeavor to produce the authority of husbands, fathers, and thence the state as mutually reinforcing and simultaneously an effort to appropriate the transgressive aspects of desire.[33] Lawrence Stone points out:

The enhancement of the importance of the conjugal family and the household relative to the kinship and clientage at the upper levels of society was accompanied by a positive reinforcement of the despotic authority of husband and father – that is to say, of patriarchy. Both Church and state provided powerful new theoretical and practical support, while two external checks on patriarchal power declined as kinship ties and clientage weakened. (*The Family, Sex and Marriage*, 151)

While the "raw power" of fathers does not necessarily increase, the recognition that such power is legitimate is fully and unequivocally established. Paternal power has now superseded "raw power" as such (151). "Authoritarian monarchy and domestic patriarchy form a congruent and mutually supportive complex of ideas and social systems" (152). As marriage was increasingly sanctified, so too was the authoritarian role of husband and father, guardian of the sacred state (654). Thus, Stone argues that after 1640, the "restricted patriarchal nuclear family becomes the "closed domesticated nuclear family" (Stone, 655).

Romeo and Juliet are simultaneously sacrificed to the old feudal order of Montague and Capulet and to patriarchy's new order of the unified power of the state represented by Escalus.[34] The play's contradictions, its combination of residual and emergent elements are subordinated by the strictures of the genre's conclusion to a single ideological effect. This does not, however, sweep away all earlier contradictions; it has taken 400 years and many times that number of pages of literary criticism to accomplish that. *Romeo and Juliet* stands as an apparently benign, lyrical document of universal love. What I have argued here is that it does not stand above history, but rather within it, doing the work of culture, instigating and perpetuating the production of socially necessary formations of desire.

When this play was written, Shakespeare was just about to begin writing the high comedies, and it fits in very well with the celebration of romantic love in those texts while it is something of an anomaly in the tragic canon. For while *Romeo and Juliet* consolidates the power of the absolutist prince as he who can take marriage alliances out of the hands of kin and promote what is to become a bourgeois family form, the tragic genre in general is unable to sustain such an ambitious and contradictory agenda. Indeed, after 1600 the increasingly retrograde cast of the tragedies is connected to their failure to imagine a synthesis of absolutism and the emerging family form. Paradoxically, however, the failure of the genre to promote the ideology of romantic love merely added cultural weight to *Romeo and Juliet*, so that it remains across the centuries the iconic text of romantic love.

Notes

1   There is in Shakespeare's play only a dim residue of this earlier moralism in the Friar's caveat that "these violent delights have violent ends" (II. vi. 9); see Bullough.

      All references to the play are to the Riverside edition, edited Evans et al.

2   For a useful guide to the literature on the debate about the transition from feudalism to capitalism, see Taylor. See also: Anderson (1979; 1983); Baechler; Baechler et al.; Brenner; Hirst; Katz; Kamenka and Neale; Medick; Mooers; Wallerstein.

3   For example, Arthur Kirsch who uses a Christian/Freudian approach comments: "Central to my understanding of the treatment of love in Shakespeare has been the assumption that the plays represent elemental truths of our emotional and spiritual life, that these truths help account for Shakespeare's enduring vitality . . ." (ix). In such criticism, Freud merely discovered a different way of expressing what Shakespeare had already said. History becomes the changing stage scenery of a continuum – the costumes may change, but the essence remains unchanged (6).

4   Even when the text was staged in a version thought more suited to the times, the result was the enhancement of its message for a post-Puritan world

wherein the ideals it presented required a certain modification. See Barnet on the theatre history of the text. The Restoration saw the popularity of a happy ending (Evans et al., 1802).

5   For Kristeva, however, such repetition is born not of ideological necessity but of a psycho-linguistic one. Commenting on the centrality of night imagery in the play, she argues: "it is not nothingness, lack of meaning, absurdity. In the polite display of its black tenderness there is an intense longing that is positive with respect to meaning . . . Let me emphasize the nocturnal motion of metaphor and *amor mortis*: it bears on the irrational aspect of signs and loving subjects, on the nonrepresentable feature on which the renewal of representation depends" (214, ellipsis in the original).

6   As Susan Amussen puts it, in nascent modernity "[b]oth economic realities and political and social thought, then, draw us to the family as a central institution" (2). Further, Sharpe points to the irrefutable arrival of one new family type: "the legitimate family of clergymen" (61).

   For debates on the family see also: Chaytor; Houlbrooke; Outhwaite; Stone.

7   "The fact, too, that in this situation he regards his father as a disturbing rival and would like to get rid of him and take his place is a straightforward consequence of the actual state of affairs" ("Some psychical consequences," 672).

8   Freud's insistence on this point leads Rosalind Coward to argue that we cannot defend the ahistoricism of Freud's theories by arguing that they are applicable to a specific, if inordinately lengthy, period of time, namely the patriarchal era (189; see also Weeks, 158–9).

9   There is a sense too in which the processes of psychoanalysis and those of conventional historiography are analogous. Freud saw himself as something of an archeologist of the psyche: "the analyst's final reconstruction of the repressed psychic life of the analysand was the objective historical truth about repressed psychic reality" (Novick, 558).

10 Even Deleuze and Guattari, who reject the oedipal construct, merely replace its universality with the fragmentation of desire, a displacement which ignores gender categories and is in danger of ignoring choice, reason, and history along with them. See Weeks, 173–6, for an excellent critique of *Anti-Oedipus*.

   For Valerie Traub, whose goal is to articulate the historical specificity of women's homoerotic desire, it is imperative "to tease out the mutually implicated but distinct relation between gender and eroticism . . . Such a project involves specifying erotic discourses and practices; describing institutional delimitations on erotic practice; detailing the resistance of subjects to the ideological and material constraints upon their erotic lives; and tracing the play of erotic discourses and practices throughout history" ("Desire and the difference it makes," 90). For this reason it is important to understand the binarism "desire and history" as ideologically constructed rather than as natural and self-evident. Jeffrey Weeks points out:

> "Desire" dances on the precipice between determinism and disruption. After Freud, it cannot be reduced to primeval biological urges, beyond human control, nor can it be seen as the product of conscious willing and planning. It is somewhere ambiguously, elusively, in between, omnipotent but tangible, powerful but goal-less. Because of this it can lay claim to universality, to being out of time and beyond identity, infiltrating the diverse spaces of our social lives, casting out delicate strands which embrace or entrap, isolate or unify. But it also has a history. The flux of desire is hooked, trapped and defined by historical processes which far from being beyond understanding, need to be understood. (157)

11   The principal objections to the use of psychoanalysis in conjunction with materialist criticism have been, as one Renaissance critic put it, that it is "ahistorical, Europocentric, and sexist . . ." (Brown, 71). (On phallocentricity see also Michael Ryan, 104–11). As a result, psychoanalysis has a complex history within the women's movement; for that matter, it has also acquired something of a troublesome geography given its very different place in British, American, and French feminist struggles. This, of course, omits Australia, another western nation which has taken Lacan to its bosom (see, for example, Grosz). There is vehement (and justifiable) antipathy to psycho-analysis among feminist activists in the American tradition of Kate Millett, which is the response to the repressive, normalizing elements of psychoanaly-sis as well as to the practices of clinical psychology (which does not adhere to the fundamental – and most radical – principles of psychoanalysis as Freud formulated them). Yet there is also a strong Francophone tradition in the US represented by, for example, Shoshana Felman, Jane Gallop, and Alice Jardine. In France, there has been opposition to Freud and Lacan (the forms of psychological theory which can properly be labelled as psychoanalytic), but it has been within the intellectual perimeters of psychoanalysis rather than a repudiation of psychoanalysis as such (Irigaray, Montrelay, Kristeva, etc.). These feminist proponents/opponents of psychoanalysis while they are vigorously political (more obviously so than their American Francophone counterparts) can hardly be described as materialists. In Britain, on the other hand, where there is a strong tradition of intellectual Marxism, psychoanaly-sis has been seen as less antithetical to materialism than elsewhere, a tendency

reinforced early on in the women's movement by Juliet Mitchell's path-breaking defence of the radical potential of psychoanalysis, *Psychoanalysis and Feminism*. However, even in Britain one can think of examples of materialist feminists who are quite opposed to psychoanalysis, for example Michèle Barrett, whose widely influential book, *Women's Oppression Today*, offers a riposte to Mitchell, and more recently Chris Weedon's *Feminism and Poststructuralism* which repeatedly delineates the shortcomings of psycho-analysis for feminism. Jane Moore and Catherine Belsey have lately argued, in a position representative of the British compromise on feminism and psychoanalysis, that psychoanalysis *versus* feminism is a reductive binarism in which "for" or "against" are the only possible positions. This is itself, they contend, a failure to historicize the role of this discussion within feminism where different questions have been asked at different historical moments. Thus, for example, ". . . Millett is concerned with the way patriarchy victim-izes women, while Mitchell and Rose are concerned with evidence that victims of patriarchy are in a position to strike back" (7).

There is, then, a pervasive sense that materialism and psychoanalysis are incompatible and yet a Marxist tradition from Trotsky, which is quite the reverse, with perhaps its most recent manifestation in Terry Eagleton's declaration that "psychoanalysis is nothing less than a materialist theory of the making of the human subject" (163). That tradition of critical engage-ment with the most radical aspects of psychoanalytic theory in Marxist criticism includes, for example, Louis Althusser's "Ideology and ideological state apparatuses" and "Freud and Lacan" (in *Lenin and Philosophy*) and Fredric Jameson's, *The Political Unconscious: Narrative as a Socially Symbolic Act*. It also includes, of course, famous attacks on psychoanalysis such as Gilles Deleuze and Félix Guattari, *Anti-Oedipus: Capitalism and Schizophrenia*. Colonial and post-colonial criticism has also engaged with psychoanalysis since it was Freud who first drew the analogy between the operations of colonialism and psychic repression (Brown, 71), and which has been taken up most power-fully by Nigerian writer, Franz Fanon in *Black Skin, White Masks*. Fanon is concerned with the political constructions of identity, and the way in which in our very psychic interiority we take up race and national identities within ideology and in the service of the hegemonic order. Similarly, Cora Kaplan has argued that this is equally true of gender and class: "Our identities are still constructed through social hierarchy and cultural differentiation, as well as those processes of division and fragmentation, described in psychoanalytic theory" (175).

To return to the specifics of the feminist tradition, there is a tension on the one hand between the desire to register the fact that constructions of gender and sexuality are historically specific (Newton and Rosenfelt, xvi) and, on the other, that certain fundamental aspects of patriarchy are stubbornly tenacious, and that they are enacted and structured even at the level of consciousness itself. Further, although gendered identities are constructed as stable, they are profoundly unstable and subject to a resistance which is at the heart of psychic life (Newton and Rosenfelt, xviii).

One of the sources of this tension, I contend, is in the desire to critique liberal humanist understandings of the subject, particularly its emphasis on the individual in the notion of an autonomous psychic interiority, which thus transcends history. Yet psychoanalysis, perhaps more than any other contemporary discourse, has effected a Copernican revolution in the sphere of the subject. The autonomous, unified coherent self of liberal humanism has been replaced by a fragmented subjectivity constituted in language rather than in some otherworldly realm of souls. Nonetheless, psychoanalysis and the "universalism" allegedly present there is unreasonably, in my view, equated with the universalizing of the liberal humanist tradition.

For a useful overview of this issues from a humanist perspective, see Gardiner.

An example of the dilemma from the perspective of feminist Renaissance studies is Valerie Traub's essay on the repressed maternal body of the history plays. She writes, "The salient difference between the Henriad and psychoanalysis . . . is less ideological than sytlistic" ("Prince Hal's Falstaff," 458). Thus Traub emphasizes the historical continuity of the phallocentric repression of the mother as a significant actor in the oedipal drama.

12 Elsewhere in the book, however, Mitchell comments, "The degree of specificity and universality has, I think, still to be worked out" (363). Addressing the argument that Freud's theories can only be applied to the nineteenth-century Vienna in which he formulated them she writes: "Certainly, then, psychoanalysis, as any other system of thought, was formed within a particular time and place; that does not invalidate its claims to universal laws, it only means that these laws have to be extracted from their specific problematic – the particular material conditions of their formation" (xviii).

13 For a summary of this debate, see Houlbrooke, chs 1 and 2.

14 For Stone's comments on developments in academic historiography, see Novick, 620.

15 The use of Foucault, let alone Freud or Lacan, is viewed as "an exercise in anachronism and dislocation" (Cressy, 125). Similarly, Cressy charges that literary scholars engage in a naïve use of the work of Lawrence Stone. However, he does not cite Mary Beth Rose's critique of Stone, which addresses the limitations but also suggests why he is useful for literary scholars who are more attuned to concepts of ideology than empiricist historians (Rose, 2–3).

In a somewhat lengthy meditation on the age of marriage in early modern England, Peter Laslett worries the question of Juliet's age (fourteen) and that of her mother (twenty-eight):

> The more the point is laboured, the less credible the view that there was anything realistic whatever in the literary intentions of the play in these respects.
>
> If we ask ourselves what those intentions were, we might suppose that Shakespeare was playing upon the rather hazy information of the bulk of his audience about the maturational differences between aristocrats and the mass of people . . . Much more plausible is the view that he was deliberately writing a play about love and marriage amongst boys and girls without any recognition of the facts about the age of women at their weddings or at sexual maturity. (*The World We Have Lost*, 85)

The reason for this, Laslett concludes, is that writers of literature have a penchant for the unusual, the out of the ordinary. He concludes that, as a result, literary evidence is almost systematically unreliable.

16   It is significant that Macfarlane ("The cradle of capitalism") is not entirely convinced of the fact that there was a transition from feudalism to capitalism. Because he can find capital in the feudal era, he questions the "supposed transition" from one mode of production to another. Macfarlane here ignores one of Marx's most fundamental definitions of capitalism. That is, "capital" always exists, but it only functions as such within specific sets of economic and social relations, just as gold has value only within particular relations.

17   Interestingly enough, it is in Lawrence Stone's *The Past and the Present* that we find the sort of unambivalent pronouncement about the (antithetical) relation between psychoanalysis and history that we would expect from a historian:

> Nothing in the historical record disproves Freud's theory about how at different stages of infantile development different erogenous zones become the foci of sexual stimulation, thus providing a logical explanation of the later relationship between oral, anal, and genital pleasure. Nor does the historical record do anything to belittle the importance of sublimation, or of the unconscious operating with a secret dynamic of its own. What it does do, however, is to cast very great doubt upon the assumption that particular kinds of infantile traumas upon which Freud laid so much stress have been suffered by the whole of the human race at all times and in all places. It is now fairly clear that four

of the main traumas Freud looked for and found among his patients, and therefore assumed to be universal, are dependent on particular experiences which did not happen to the vast majority of people in most of the recorded past, but which were peculiar to middle-class urban culture of late Victorian Europe. (216–17)

18   For a related account of resistance to Continental thought and to African-American and feminist historiography, see Novick, especially chs 14 and 15.
19   Alice Jardine notes: "In contemporary French thought, it is not the "event" that assumes importance as a historical mark, but the epistemological configurations surrounding that event, especially with regard to language" (82–3). Also, it is worth pointing out that the problem of legitimation addressed by Lyotard and the problem of knowledge articulated by Foucault are, then, "historical" problems with the very idea of history itself.
20   Psychoanalysis, at least in Greenblatt's rendition of it, threatens to ground history in identity:

If psychoanalysis was, in effect, made possible by (among other things) the legal and literary proceedings of the sixteenth and seventeenth centuries, then its interpretive practice is not irrelevant to those proceedings, nor is it exactly an anachronism. But psychoanalysis is causally belated, even as it is causally linked: hence the curious effect of a discourse that functions *as if* the psychological categories it invokes were not only simultaneous with but even prior to and themselves causes of the very phenomena of which in actual fact they were the results. (221)

Of course, Greenblatt has himself very effectively deployed psychoanalysis in his treatment of desire in *Othello* in *Renaissance Self-Fashioning*. He writes:

Shakespeare's military hero, it may be objected, is particularly far removed from this introspective project, a project that would seem, in any case, to have little bearing upon any Renaissance text. Yet I think it is no accident that nearly every phase of Lacan's critique of psychoanalysis seems a brilliant reading of Othello, for I would propose that there is a deep resemblance between the construction of the self in analysis – at least as Lacan conceives it – and Othello's self-fashioning. The resemblance is grounded in the dependence of even the innermost self upon a language that is always necessarily given from without and upon representation before an audience. I do not know if such are the

conditions of human identity, apart from its expression in psychoanalysis, but they are unmistakably the conditions of theatrical identity, where existence is conferred upon a character by the playwright's
language and the actor's performance. (244–5)

21   It is not of course that undecidability can never be intellectually productive,
whatever its political limitations. For example, Greenblatt comments
"'psyche' is neither a mere mystification for 'property' nor a radical alternative to it" ("Psychoanalysis and Renaissance Culture," 224; see also 220–1).

22   Because of his immensely influential pioneering work in the field, there is
something of a danger of equating new historicism with Greenblatt alone.
Other new historicists such as Louis Montrose and Don Wayne are rather
more concerned with class and gender struggles as motivating historical
contestation. Undoubtedly also, Geenblatt has exerted a powerful (and for
that matter positive) effect on scholarship which is explicitly Marxist and
feminist. See Howard; Montrose; Veeser; Wayne.

23   While it would be naïve to claim a straightforward functional relation
between the nuclear family and the capitalist mode of production, it would
fly in the face of historical fact to ignore the changes in familial structure and
function that the changing organization effected. The degree of debate about
this shift cannot be overemphasized. It is difficult to offer empirical evidence
for changing family forms. However, Stone notes the fact that in the four-
teenth century only a small proportion of homicides were committed within
the family, in comparison with the majority today: "What is so striking,
however, is that the family was more a unit for the perpetuation of crime –
a third of all group crimes were by family members – than a focus of crime.
It is tempting to argue that the family that slayed together stayed together"
(*The Family, Sex and Marriage*, 95). Even on a less lethal level, community
interactions seem to have revolved around identification with a larger unit
than the one we think of as the nuclear family. "[E]verything we know about
the pre-modern community, such as the village, indicates that it was riddled
with competitive feuds and factions, usually organized around kinship
groups" (660).

24   In contrast, psychoanalytic readings of the play, even as they demonstrate the
way feudal patriarchy naturalizes itself, themselves succumb to that natural-
ization, accepting its self-representation as static and monolithic. For example, Copélia Kahn argues that *Romeo and Juliet* demonstrates a certain
inevitability or fate as intrinsic to the feudal patriarchal scheme which
produces such strain on the young people who must come of age in Verona
(186).

25   For the family was the central unit of most production as much as it was a

institution of ideological importance for social and political theory and "the domestic relations of the household were an explicit part of the production relations of early capitalism" (Zaretsky, 38). "[P]roperty was a central factor in family relations, from decisions to get married to the distribution of property at the time of death (Amussen, 94).

In a similar vein, Immanuel Wallerstein argues

> . . . the image of historical capitalism having arisen via the overthrow of a backward aristocracy by a progressive bourgeoisie is wrong. Instead, the correct basic image is that historical capitalism was brought into existence by a landed aristocracy which transformed itself into a bourgeoisie because the old system was disintegrating. Rather than let the disintegration continue to uncertain ends, they engaged in radical structural surgery themselves in order to maintain and significantly expand their ability to exploit the direct producers. (105–6)

26 "When verbal sparring about phalluses turns into physical sparring with swords, Mercutio is killed. An exemplar of male violence and misogyny? A martyr to male friendship? A victim of sexual desire that he cannot, will not, or must not acknowledge directly? Mercutio is all three" (Smith, 64).

27 On the violence of male bonding see: Kahn, 82–118; Novy, 99–142; Smith, ch. 2.

28 Notably, the fathers loom so large in the play in Stockholder's psychoanalytic interpretation that she views Capulet as the protagonist (31).

29 In fact the incest taboo is more vulnerable when it operates in the tense nuclear arrangement where any affective relations outside the nuclear unit are discouraged and deemed inappropriate (see Mitchell, *Psychoanalysis and Feminism*). Yet in this play, it is the feudal that is presented as an aberrant way of organizing desire, as perverted and death-marked.

30 "Nevertheless, the dramatic representation of that [neo-Catholic] sensibility is at its most commanding and pristine in Elizabethan, rather than in Jacobean, tragedy" (Rose, 105).

31 For Kay Stockholder the threat to the couple is externalized: "The freer the lovers are from violent emotions, the more violent is the world they encounter" (30). And for Kiernan Ryan the play represents a subversive utopian vision, born of an initial freedom from social identity (a namelessness), cruelly dashed (108, 114, 117). Ryan suggests that the play is revolutionary and argues for a love untrammeled by the social order. Such a suggestion seems beside the point – love is always, first and foremost, social.

Kristeva considers the couple a "utopic wager that paradise lost can be made lasting" (222), but this is exactly the dominant ideology of love in modernity, and it is for Kristeva a utopian option she rejects out of hand where authority constitutes itself as that which is to be loved (210).

32 Stone argues that there is a "clear conflict: between romantic love and the notion that it is an impractical basis for marriage" (*The Family, Sex and Marriage*, 181). I disagree because it seems to me that "romantic love," the ideal of a love between equals (that is, people of the same class status), is one of the most successful ways of internalizing the social order – that is, producing it in socially appropriate ways.

33 Alan Sinfield remarks: "The . . . disjunction in Reformation doctrine of marriage occurred because theorists wanted to maintain, as well as the husband's authority, the father's. They did not mean to let their young folk get out of hand, or to let human feeling supplant the other important things in life. The ideal of affectionate marriage was held alongside a continuing belief in parental control, mainly in the interests of social standing and financial security" (7).

34 John Donne in one of his typically perverse wedding sermons, proclaims that proper godliness should obviate desire and obliterate lack: "And what can that soul lack that hath all God?" (Rose, 104). The state of fulfillment, a state beyond desire, is envisaged here. A perfect Christianity, it would seem, obliterates lack, that precondition of desire produced by an initial failure of satisfaction and as the effect of a primordial absence. Donne reduces sexual desire back to the order of a need; something that could be satisfied (see J. Rose, "Introduction II" to Mitchell and Rose, 32).

Works Cited

Althusser, Louis, *Lenin and Philosophy and Other Essays*, trans. Ben Brewster (New York, Monthly Review Press, 1971).

Amussen, Susan Dwyer, *An Ordered Society: Gender and Class in Early Modern England* (Oxford, Basil Blackwell, 1988).

Anderson, Perry, *Lineages of the Absolutist State* (London, Verso, 1979).

——, *In the Tracks of Historical Materialism* (London, Verso, 1983).

Baechler, Jean, *The Origins of Capitalism*, trans. Barry Cooper (Oxford, Basil Blackwell, 1975).

Baechler, Jean, Hall, John, and Mann, Michael, *Europe and the Rise of Capitalism* (Oxford, Basil Blackwell, 1988).

Barnet, Sylvan, "*Romeo and Juliet* on stage and screen," in J. A. Bryant (ed.), *The Tragedy of Romeo and Juliet*, The Signet Classic Shakespeare (New York, Penguin, 1986), 227–38.

Barrett, Michèle, *Women's Oppression Today* (London, Verso, 1980).

Barrett, Michèle and McIntosh, Mary, *The Anti-Social Family* (London, Verso, 1982).

Belsey, Catherine and Moore, Jane (eds), *The Feminist Reader: Essays in Gender and the Politics of Literary Criticism* (Cambridge, MA, Basil Blackwell, 1989).

Brenner, Robert, "The Origins of capitalist development: a critique of neo-Smithian Marxism," *New Left Review*, 104 (1977), 25–92.

Brown, Paul, " 'This thing of darkness I acknowledge mine': *The Tempest* and the discourse of colonialism," in Jonathan Dollimore and Alan Sinfield (eds), *Political Shakespeare: New Essays in Cultural Materialism* (Ithaca, Cornell University Press, 1985), 48–71.

Bullough, Geoffrey (ed.), *Narrative and Dramatic Sources of Shakespeare*, vol. 1 (New York, Columbia University Press, 1957).

Chaytor, Miranda, "Household and kinship: Ryton in the late sixteenth and early seventeenth centuries," *History Workshop Jounnal*, 10 (1980), 25–60.

Coward, Rosalind, *Patriarchal Precedents: Sexuality and Social Relations* (Boston, Routledge & Kegan Paul, 1983).

Cressy, David, "Foucault, Stone, Shakespeare, and social history," *English Literary Renaissance*, 21(2) (1991), 121–33.

Davies, Kathleen M., "Continuity and change in literary advice on marriage," in R. B. Outhwaite (ed.), *Marriage and Society: Studies in the Social History of Marriage* (New York, St Mantiu's Press, 1981).

Deleuze, Gilles and Guattari, Félix, *Anti-Oedipus: Capitalism and Schizophrenia*, trans. Robert Hurley et al. (Minneapolis, University of Minnesota Press, 1983).

Eagleton, Terry, *Literary Theory; An Introduction* (Oxford, Basil Blackwell, 1983).

Evans, G. Blakemore et al. (ed.), *The Riverside Shakespeare* (Boston, Houghton Mifflin, 1974).

Fanon, Franz, *Black Skins, White Masks*, trans. Charles Lam Markmann (New York, Grove Press, 1967).

Freud, Sigmund, *Moses and Monotheism* (1939), trans. Katherine Jones (New York, Vintage, 1962).

——, *Totem and Taboo: Resemblances between the Psychic Lives of Savages and Neurotics*, in Peter Gay (ed.), *The Freud Reader* (New York, Nonton, 1989), 481–513.

——, "Some psychical consequences of the anatomical distinction between the sexes," in Peter Gay (ed.), *The Freud Reader* (New York, Nonton, 1989), 670–7.

Gardiner, Judith Kegan, "Psychoanalysis and feminism: an American humanist's view," *Signs*, 17 (winter 1992), 437–54.

Gibbons, Brian (ed.), *Romeo and Juliet*, the Arden Shakespeare (London, Methuen, 1980).

Greenblatt, Stephen, *Renaissance Self-Fashioning from More to Shakespeare* (Chicago, University of Chicago Press, 1980).

——, "Psychoanalysis and Renaissance culture," in Patricia Parker and David Quint (eds), *Literary Theory/Renaissance Texts* (Baltimore, Johns Hopkins, 1986), 210–24.

Grosz, Elizabeth, *Jacques Lacan: A Feminist Introduction* (New York, Routledge, 1990).

Hirst, Paul Q., *Marxism and Historical Writing* (London, Routledge, 1985).

Houlbrooke, Ralph A., *The English Family, 1450–1700* (New York, Longman, 1988).

Howard, Jean, "The New Historicism in Renaissance studies," *English Literary Renaissance*, 16(1) (winter, 1986), 13–43.

Jameson, Frederic, *The Ideologies of Theory: Essays 1971–1986*, vol. 1 (Minneapolis, University of Minnesota Press, 1981).

——, *The Political Unconscious: Narrative as a Socially Symbolic Act* (Ithaca, Cornell University Press, 1985).

Jardine, Alice, *Gynesis: Configurations of Woman and Modernity* (Ithaca, Cornell University Press, 1985).

Jones, Barry, "Romeo and Juliet: the genesis of a classic," in Eric Haywood and Cormac Ó Cuilleanáin (eds), *Italian Storytellers: Essays on Italian Narrative Literature* (Dublin, Irish Academic Press, 1989), 150–81.

Kahn, Coppélia, *Man's Estate: Masculine Identity in Shakespeare* (Berkeley, University of California Press, 1981).

Kamenka, Eugene and Neale, R. S., *Feudalism, Capitalism and Beyond* (London, Edward Arnold, 1975).

Kaplan, Cora, *Sea Changes: Culture and Feminism* (London, Verso, 1986).

Katz, Claudio J., *From Feudalism to Capitalism: Marxian Theories of Class Struggle and Social Change* (New York, Greenwood Press, 1989).

Kirsch, Arthur, *Shakespeare and the Experience of Love* (New York, Cambridge University Press, 1981).

Kristeva, Julia, *Tales of Love*, trans. Leon S. Roudiez (New York, Columbia University Press, 1987).

Laslett, Peter, *The World We Have Lost Further Explored* (London, Methuen, 1965, 1983).

——, "The European family and early Industrialization," in Jean Baechler et al. (eds), 234–41.

Macfarlane, Alan, Review of Lawrence Stone's *The Family, Sex and Marriage in England, History and Theory*, 18 (1979), 103–26.

——, *Marriage and Love in England: Modes of Reproduction 1300–1840* (Oxford, Basil Blackwell, 1986).

——, "The cradle of capitalism: the case of England," in Jean Baechler et al. (eds), 185–203.

Marx, Karl and Engels, Friedrich, *The Marx–Engels Reader*, ed. Robert C. Tucker (New York, Norton, 1978).

Medick, Hans. "The transition from feudalism to capitalism: renewal of the debate," in Raphael Samuel (ed.) *People's History and Socialist Theory* (London, Routledge & Kegan Paul, 1981).

Mitchell, Juliet, *Woman's Estate* (New York, Vintage, 1973).

——, *Psychoanalysis and Feminism: Freud, Reich, Laing and Women* (New York, Vintage, 1975).

Mitchell, Juliet and Rose, Jacqueline, *Feminine Sexuality: Feminine Sexuality and the ecole freudienne*, trans. Jacqueline Rose (London, Macmillan, 1982).

Montrose, Louis, "Renaissance literary studies and the subject of history," *English Literary Renaissance*, 16(1) (1986), 5–12.

Mooers, Colin, *The Making of Bourgeois Europe: Absolutism, Revolution, and the Rise of Capitalism in England, France, and Germany* (New York, Verso, 1991).

Mooney, Michael, "Text and performance: *Romeo and Juliet*, Quartos 1 and 2," *Colby Quarterly*, XXVI(2) (June 1990), 122–32.

Newman, Karen, *Fashioning Femininity and English Renaissance Drama* (Chicago, University of Chicago Press, 1991).

Newton, Judith and Rosenfelt, Deborah (eds), *Feminist Literary Criticism and Social Change* (New York, Routledge, 1986).

Novick, Peter, *That Noble Dream: The 'Objectivity Question" and the American Historical Profession* (Cambridge, Cambridge University Press, 1988).

Novy, Marianne, *Love's Argument: Gender Relations in Shakespeare* (Chapel Hill, University of North Carolina Press, 1984).

Outhwaite, R. B. (ed.), *Marriage and Society: Studies in the Social History of Marriage* (New York, St Martin's Press, 1981).

Porter, Joseph, "Marlowe, Shakespeare, and the canonization of heterosexuality," *South Atlantic Quarterly*, 88(1) (1989), 127–47.

Rose, Mary Beth, *The Expense of Spirit: Love and Sexuality in English Renaissance Drama* (Ithaca, Cornell University Press, 1988).

Rougement, Denis de, *Love in the Western World*, trans. Montgomery Belgion (Princeton, NJ: Princeton University Press, 1983).

Ryan, Kiernan, "*Romeo and Juliet*: the language of tragedy," in Willie van Peer (ed.), *Taming the Text* (New York, Routledge, 1988), 106–21.

Ryan, Michael, *Marxism and Deconstruction* (Baltimore, Johns Hopkins, 1982).

Sharpe, J. A., *Early Modern England: A Social History 1550–1760* (London, Edward Arnold, 1987).

Sinfield, Alan, *Literature in Protestant England, 1560–1660* (Towota, NJ, Barnes & Noble, 1983).

Smith, Bruce R., *Homosexual Desire in Shakespeare's England: A Cultural Poetics* (Chicago, University of Chicago Press, 1991).

Stockholder, Kay, *Dreamworks: Lovers and Families in Shakespeare's Plays* (Toronto, University of Toronto Press, 1987).

Stone, Lawrence, *The Family, Sex and Marriage in England 1500–1800* (New York, Harper & Row, 1977).

——, *The Past and the Present* (Boston, Routledge & Kegan Paul, 1980).

Swindells, Julia and Jardine, Lisa, *What's Left? Women in Culture and the Labour Movement* (New York, Routledge, 1990).

Taylor, Barry, *Society and Economy in Early Modern Europe: A Bibliography of Post-War Research* (New York, Manchester University Press, 1989).

Traub, Valerie, "Kay Stockholder. *Dream works: lovers and families in Shakespeare's plays,*" *Shakespeare Quarterly*, 40(1) (spring 1989), 100–2.

——, "Prince Hal's Falstaff: positioning psychoanalysis and the female reproductive Body," *Shakespeare Quarterly*, 40(4) (1989), 456–74.

——, "Desire and the difference it makes," in Valerie Wayne (ed.), *The Matter of Difference: Materialist Feminist Criticism of Shakespeare* (Ithaca, Cornell, 1991), 81–114.

Veeser, Aram H. (ed.), *The New Historicism* (New York, Routledge, 1989).

Wallerstein, Immanuel, *Historical Capitalism* (London, Verso, 1983).

Wayne, Don E., "New historicism," in Martin Coyle, Peter Garside, Malcolm Kelsall, and John Peck (eds), *Encyclopedia of Literature and Criticism* (London, Routledge, 1990).

Weedon, Chris, *Feminism and Poststructuralism* (London, Routledge, 1989).

Weeks, Jeffrey, *Sexuality and its Discontents: Meanings, Myths, and Modern Sexualities* (London, Routledge, 1985).

Whittier, Gayle, "The sonnet's body and the body sonnetized in *Romeo and Juliet,*" *Shakespeare Quarterly*, 40(1) (spring 1989), 27–41.

Wrightson, Keith, *English Society 1580–1680* (New Brunswick, NJ, Rutgers University Press, 1982).

Zaretsky, Eli, *Capitalism, the Family and Personal Life* (London, Pluto, 1976).

3

Acts of Resistance

The Feminist Player

Lorraine Helms

> There's language in her eye, her cheek, her lip.
> Nay, her foot speaks; her wanton spirits look out
> At every joint and motive of her body.
> O, these encounterers, so glib of tongue,
> That give a coasting welcome ere it comes,
> And wide unclasp the tables of their thoughts,
> To every ticklish reader! set them down
> For sluttish spoils of opportunity,
> And daughters of the game.
> *Troilus and Cressida*, IV. v. 55–63

The words are Ulysses', the legible body is Cressida's and the scene is her entrance into the Greek camp, where she has just been kissed in turn by each of the generals. Although the dramaturgy of the scene seems to grant misogyny the privilege of choric comment, feminist critics have challenged Ulysses, arguing that he is himself a "ticklish reader," not an omniscient narrator. They have also criticized a theatrical tradition that conflates Ulysses' utterance with authorial instructions for staging the scene.[1]

While critics and historians, gazing from house to stage, have watched Ulysses' attempts to transform Cressida's body into a pornographic image, feminist players, glancing from stage to house, have confronted the directors and designers who demand that they embody Ulysses' text.[2] These parallels between the player's and the scholar's work anticipate the collaborations between theatrical practice and critical discourse on which the project of this chapter depends.

Within the microcosmic anthropology of Shakespearean performance, player and scholar frequently become the other's Other. While players scoff at the arid quiddities of the academy, they fear lest historical research reveal a veridical bard that they cannot incarnate. While scholars shudder at the gawdy vulgarities of the entertainment industry, they envy the commitment of lives lived in the theatre. Even in performance criticism, where anti-theatrical pride and prejudice do not deride the interpretive community of players, scholars have often turned theatre into the site of ethnographic adventures and players into native informants, meeting their perspective variously with contempt, dismay, deference, or adulation. But the canon and the repertory are threads woven into the same fabric: the creation of a feminist Cressida in the twentieth century is only one instance of the resemblance that the records of stage and study come to reveal even a few years on. I do not intend to deny distinctions between the practices of the theatre and the professions of criticism. Indeed, I shall often insist on them. Yet these distinctions, less absolute than antitheses, should not sabotage shared goals.

In this chapter, then, I want to look from house to stage and from stage to house, considering both the playgoer's pleasure and the player's job of work. The first section, "Embodying the Text," asks whether the contemporary Shakespearean actress enjoys the transhistorical privileges and prerogatives that Michael Goldman calls "the actor's freedom." While social sanctions, theatrical occasions, and dramatic fictions may all qualify the player's perfect liberty, Goldman's phenomenology of playing does help to locate the area within which the player makes her interpretive choices.

To explore this area, the next two sections focus on soliloquy. Soliloquy concentrates theatrical energy on the relation between player and audience, enhancing the player's opportunities to affect the meaning of the representation. First, "Playing the Woman's Part" describes conventions of the soliloquy that favored the adults over the boys in Shakespeare's company and the clowns over the women in his plays. The next section, "Playing the Clown," seeks ways to reinterpret those conventions in the contemporary theatre. I concentrate on the monologues of three women's roles: Joan of Arc, from *1 Henry VI*; Cressida; and the Jailer's Daughter, from *The Two Noble Kinsmen*. In each, what I shall call the politics of prosody reveal certain tantalizing affinities with the soliloquies of the clown.

In writing about these soliloquies, I attempt to translate into critical discourse some discoveries I have made when "embodying the text." I also want to ask how such discoveries fare in the achieved *mises en scène* of mainstream Shakespearean performance, and the next section, "Playing the Boy's Part," reviews several recent interpretations of these characters and their soliloquies. The final three sections, "The Theatricality of Witchcraft," "Tragical–Comical–Pastoral–Historical–Mythical–Musical *Macbeth*," and "The Weyward Sisters Go on Tour" explore possibilities for incorporating feminist theory and stage history into Shakespearean performance. Moving from history to hypothesis, I conclude with the sketch of an imaginary production of *Macbeth*.

Embodying the Text

Who is the audience; who is the performer? They pay; we don't. That makes them the johns; we are the dancing girls. The real difference: we are prepared, they aren't.

Judith Malina

Cressida can resist Ulysses' attempt to translate her body into the discourses of patriarchy only through gesture, posture, and inflection. These languages of physical presence center her commitment to the play text in her own body, with all its laggardly knowledge, ancient grudges, and new mutinies. Although the feminist critic can enfranchise the playgoer by tracing the treacherous silences and errors that would otherwise entrap her, the player cannot thus evade the corporeal exaltations and abasements of text and tradition. She cannot resort to a "negative" feminism and say with Julia Kristeva, " 'that's not it' and 'that's still not it' " (137).[3] She must have grounds more relative than this, for she must choose, moment by moment, word by word, gesture by gesture, to *do* something.

But if text and tradition demand that the feminist player enact the oppression of women, can she enjoy what Michael Goldman calls the actor's freedom? "While on stage, the actor enjoys a kind of omnipotence, a privilege and protection not unlike that accorded sacred beings – whatever he is doing, whatever crimes he may appear to commit, he is not to be interfered with. Yet at the same time he seems abnormally exposed, abnormally dependent upon us" (9). While Goldman acknowledges that the freedom of this implicitly male player entails psychological risk, he neglects the social, political, legal, and economic foundations of historical theatre practices. Only thus can one imagine a stage that offers such full immunity from the sanctions of the surrounding culture.

For Herbert Blau, those sanctions nullify any histrionic "privilege and protection": "The actor's freedom," he counters, "has always been – given the emarginated history of the profession – the most pathetic illusion" (314). Indeed, history has on occasion ruthlessly quashed the player's transhistorical freedom. The Roman actor assassinated on stage to satisfy the emperor's craving for realism, the Elizabethan schoolboy impressed into service as a chorister in the queen's chapel, and the pornographic film star repeatedly raped on camera are players whose liberty is violently annuled in a pyrrhic victory of life over art.[4]

Even the stages that effectively exclude such dangers cannot elude the symbolic violence of representation. Scripts, settings, costume and casting, directorial commands and caveats, the demography and disposition of the audience, and even the half-remembered relics of abandoned conventions – masks and buskins and boys who play the woman's part – may free the actor or entrap him. Social and sexual hierarchies reemerge from within the dramatic fiction and the theatrical occasion to shape the interacting subjectivities of player and player, player and spectator.

Nor does the actor's "emarginated history" fully disclose the historical vulnerabilities of the actress. His mask, the Greek *persona*, enters our very idea of a person; her mask is the prostitute's vizard. Her freedom is forfeited in Renaissance England, and whenever law or custom keep her from the stage. It is jeopardized in Restoration England, when her theatrical roles fuse with the role her profession plays in commodifying the female body.[5]

In the theatrical cultures of the twentieth century, she has become a yet more diversified commodity. "The prima donna," Catherine Clément remarks in *Opéra; or, the Undoing of Women*, "has to appear the way men want her, like that other woman dressed up as a woman, Norma Jean, who was called Marilyn Monroe. And there is a lot of writhing about them. Feathers, eyes rimmed by false lashes, artificial blondness, whimsy, and a body dressed as a woman" (29). Conversely, Balanchine ballerinas become female impersonators by repressing the voluptuousness that the prima donna and film star cultivate, prolonging nubility at the cost of "the distortions of exaggerated turnout and *pointe*, the misalignments working their way up the spine . . . the stressed ligaments and joints, the slow anorexic diminution of the flesh" (Roach, 116). What seems for Goldman's actor "abnormal" exposure and dependence may for a female performer merely corroborate the quotidian fictions of femininity.

Like the prima donna, the ballerina, and the film star, the Shakespearean actress obeys rigorous rules for female impersonation. In "Representing Ophelia: women, madness, and the responsibilities of feminist criticism," Elaine Showalter argues optimistically that "when Shakespeare's heroines began to be played by women instead of boys, the presence of the female body and female voice, quite apart from details of interpretation, created new meanings and subversive tensions in these roles" (80). But within theatrical structures largely controlled by masculinist directors, producers, designers, and promoters, the energies of the female voice and body are readily channelled into ventriloquism. The history of the twentieth-century directors' theatre, like that of the eighteenth- and nineteenth-century theatre of the actor-manager, reveals revisions, excisions, and interpolations that diminish and distort female roles.[6]

Even barring such directorial interventions, the Shakespearean stage, restricting the number of female characters, the time they spend on stage, and the company they keep, demands that the actress risk rather more the actor. "You are often the only woman in the rehearsal room," Fiona Shaw remarks: "The Kate I played in *The Shrew* was a direct product of the rehearsal process. I was conscious of wanting to radiate the sense of terribly clouded confusion that overwhelms you when you are the only woman around. That was Kate's position, and it was mine" (Rutter, xvii). A woeful Cressid among the merry Greeks, Kate (and Shaw) must suffer this solitude in silence: "But the problem with expressing any of this is that Kate doesn't have the language, she doesn't have the lines" (8).

The Shakespearean stage, then, has not liberated the actress from the restrictions of patriarchal narrative, the insults of masculinist theatre practices, or the cultural coercions that voyeurism exacts and exhibitionism accords. Less optimistic (or more radical) critics of the dramatic canon than Showalter have argued that female roles originally written by men for male performers – the Medeas and Antigones of the Greek theatre as well as the Rosalinds and Cleopatras of Shakespeare's – are caricatures, and that they should again be played by men to emphasize the fact that the classic roles are, in Sue-Ellen Case's phrase, "classic drag" (5).

Whatever the salutary effects of such casting, a feminist project that prohibits the participation of women prefigures a theoretical impasse and a practical disaster. For a feminist who wishes to make her living in the theatre, Showalter's view retains certain obvious attractions. Shakespeare is not only a metaphorical site of social meanings, but a job of work.[7] To contribute to the meanings one must accept the job of work. Like Blau, I want to acknowledge the conditions that constrain the socially and economically marginal actor and especially the sexually segregated actress. Yet I would not dismiss Goldman's insight into the phenomenology of playing. Rather, I want to argue for a freedom – however partial, problematic, and paradoxical – that remains after all these constraints have been acknowledged.

This irrevocable freedom depends on the ontological difference between theatre and the theatricality of everyday life – a difference that critical discourse has often obscured.[8] For the playgoer (and the critic of theatrical or cultural performances), there is a metaphoric relation between theatre and theatricality. Antiquity and the Renaissance recognize the resemblance in remarking the *theatrum mundi*; psychoanalysis elaborates its contemporary significance in tropes of masquerade.[9] But the metaphor of the *theatrum mundi* does not illuminate the *mundus theatrum*. For the player, the relation is also metonymic. However much a theatrical role may resonate metaphorically with one's personal and political metadramas, its most immediate meaning lies in the ways it touches one's existence, tailoring rhythms and relationships to the work at hand. Unlike the consequences that pursue cultural performances in everyday life, those of theatrical representation lie outside the logic of the enacted narrative. To reassert the simple distinction that sophisticated explorations of everyday theatricality have blurred: playing Joan of Arc will temporarily set the schedule of one's daily activities; it may permanently change the practice of one's craft and the course of one's career. It may indeed entail exploitation through any of the varied forms of sexual harassment that the actress is heir to. But it rarely leaves burn marks.

The difference is not only that the player, as the seventeenth-century "Character of an Actor" has it, does "fainedly" what others do "essentially" (Chambers, iv, 258), but that only in the theatre does faining become acting: "In acting," remarks Jan Kott, "we are many, in simulation we are divided. In acting one body has many souls; in simulation, the soul has various bodies" (14). Theatre bestows multiplicity; the theatricality of everyday life avows fragmentation.

The player's work turns pathos into praxis. When grief is enacted rather than endured, it becomes a task and an achievement. For whatever they signify to the spectator, moments of onstage pain and danger can be experienced as pleasurable; gestures of submission can be empowering and destruction creative. Imogen Stubbs, whose work I shall return to, remarks that she found it "terribly exciting" to be fitted for a crown when playing Isabel in *Richard II*, as she did being fitted for the bridle she wore when playing the mad scenes of the Jailer's Daughter in *The Two Noble Kinsmen* (54).[10] These sentiments seem to evince naïve neglect of the masculine fantasies for which such props are fashioned. Yet they rely less on the fictive premises of the representation than on the liberatory properties of play. Where the spectator may see the Shakespearean *mise en scène*, like the camera, reduce the actress to the passivity that Laura Mulvey (in a phrase so full of burrs that it has caught the petticoats of those who walk not in the trodden paths) calls "to-be-looked-at-ness" (62), the player may experience something more like "on-stage-ness," the concentrated energy of playing that cultural performances, in their consequentiality, inevitably dissipate.

I introduce "on-stage-ness" in an effort to adapt the insights of film theory to the phenomenology of Shakespearean performance. Kathleen McLuskie, among others, suggests that Shakespearean textual cues, like cinematic cues, construct the female as the object of the male spectator's gaze. As "the products of an entertainment industry which, as far as we know, had no women shareholders, writers, actors, or stage hands" (92), the play texts "resist feminist manipulation by denying an autonomous position for the female viewer of the action" (95).

Theatre, even illusionist theatre, cannot equal cinematic control over the spectator. Nor can it so effortlessly reduce the player to the unresisting receptivity of the photographic image. Still, McLuskie's comparison, insisting that critics acknowledge the textual traces of women's original exclusion from the Shakespearean stage, implicitly demands that the actress confront continuity between apparently antithetical theatrical practices. Since women now, as boys then, must play their parts in societies where women share children's disenfranchisement, physical difference continues to reflect the hierarchy of male and non-male in Shakespearean roles. Techniques originally designed to feminize the boy actor may infantilize or eroticize those who now play his roles. They may turn women, like boys, into female impersonators.

Playing the Woman's Part

First my fear, then my curtsey, then my speech.
2 Henry IV, Epilogue

The boy actors who played the woman's part in Elizabethan playhouses have left textual traces that have long engrossed (and vexed) critical speculation. Cross-casting marks the ephemeral nexus of character and player in subtle and shifting ways that historical inquiry cannot recover. The performance of the boy actor could have been erotically charged for some spectators, aesthetically distanced for others. It could have been illusionistic at one moment, only to be broken by self-reflexive theatricality at another. The femininity it imposed on male bodies could have illuminated the cultural construction of gender and at the same time have trivialized women's social roles in puerile caricatures. It could have celebrated female heroism even while relentlessly excluding women from the economic and expressive opportunities of theatrical activity.

However varied the effects of his performance, the boy actor's presumed inadequacies have traditionally been blamed for Katherine's silence, the absence of Queen Lear, and other irremediable deficiencies in Shakespeare's roles for women.[11] Theatre historians have been more voluble than the historical record in describing these inadequacies, yet the play texts do register the passage of the boy actor. For in restricting women's roles, Shakespeare's stage does not simply hold the mirror up to a society that devalues women's activities or denies them freedom of movement. Rather, it reveals its dependence on the narrowed range of difference at its disposal. For an all-male acting company, the contrast between a boy and a grown man fortifies the fiction of female presence.

This fiction need not be equated with the illusionism of later theatrical tradition. In the most rigorously conventionalized Noh plays, as in America's most casually naturalistic kitchen-sink drama, age, ethnicity, status, and gender must be represented through visual and aural differences. To place a boy on stage alone in soliloquy or accompanied only by other boys in a scene for two or more women is to relinquish or at least diminish the differences of size, vocal range, and musculature on which his feminization partly depends. During such moments, the fiction of femininity is vulnerable unless poetic, rhetorical, and narrative devices undertake the task that the adult actor performs in other scenes. Soliloquies, therefore, designed for delivery at moments when the boy actor was most independent of the shareholders and journeymen, test the textual limits to the freedom of Shakespeare's women.

Soliloquy, as Raymond Williams remarks, is a problematic term. Traditionally associated with "private meditation and reverie," in the nineteenth century it was assimilated to a Romantic characterology that has ever since obscured the varied forms of the Shakespearean monologue. In Williams's typology, these forms include the presentational, expository, and homiletic discourse of direct address; semi-direct address, which includes asides and utterances that characterize the speaker; and indirect address, the meditations and speculations that Williams calls rhetorical, reflexive, and generic. Indirect address most closely approximates the modern conception of the psychological soliloquy; it is most readily assimilated to representational playing (*Writing in Society*, 42–3). Despite these philological difficulties, I want to retain the term soliloquy to describe a solo, a presentational speech during some part of which the speaker is either alone on stage or at least not fully engaged with other players.

In *Shakespeare and the Popular Tradition*, Robert Weimann documents the place of the Shakespearean soliloquy in the tradition of presentational theatre. The Elizabethan playhouse retains the medieval distinction between the illusionistic *locus*, whence Illyria, Arden, and Elsinore will come, and the interactive *platea*, an unlocalized and nonrepresentational downstage space. This space belongs to the morality play Vice, who bequeathes it to the Shakespearean clown. From it, the clown addresses the spectators directly, mediating "between fiction and reality, the drama and the social occasion" (157). He plays a role, but more importantly he plays the crowd, addressing it in the heteroglossia of proverbs, puns, and rhyming couplets to create a comic and even carnivalesque perspective on the dramatic fiction. This tradition of direct address privileges the perspectives of clownish serving-men, porters, and gravediggers. It also safeguards the space from which heroes and villains speak their soliloquies. Aaron, Richard III, Iago, and Hamlet all borrow theatrical vitality from the Vice, while they refine his boisterous discourse into the mimesis of subjectivity.[12]

In the soliloquies of such characters, the residual choric possibilities of the *platea* mingle with new poetic devices that create the illusion of interiority: "In conjunction with the more or less contemporaneous development of the iambic pentameter," Catherine Belsey argues, "the soliloquy makes audible the personal voice and offers access to the presence of an individual speaker" (42). The iambic rhythms of interiority only partly displace the heteroglossia of the *platea*, enabling the Shakespearean soliloquy to serve the range of purposes that Williams catalogues. As the soliloquizing player moves between *locus* and *platea*, he may create a dramatic fiction or comment on the theatrical occasion; he may construct an illusion of interiority or play the crowd.

This movement contributes to the resilient multiplicity of the Shakespearean play texts, allowing twentieth-century productions an analogous range from Stanislavskian naturalism through the Brechtian *gestus*. The analogy is rough, for while the *locus* is the distant ancestor of naturalism, the metatheatrical *platea* does not anticipate Brecht's reaction to the proscenium. Only after the fourth wall has been built can breaching it shock or alienate or *épater le bourgeoisie*. Nor, despite Brecht's delight in zanies and mountebanks, can his own rigorously disciplined narratives endure the clown's improvisational interventions into the plot.[13] Nevertheless, this analogy between a Stanislavskian descendent of the *locus* and a Brechtian reinterpretation of the *platea* does at least open negotiations between the historical realities of the Elizabethan playhouse and the artistic requirements of the twentieth-century stage.

With some exceptions, Shakespeare's female characters play their roles in the illusionistic scenes of the *locus*. They enjoy few opportunities to express the interiority of the reflexive soliloquy and even fewer to address the audience from the interactive *platea*.[14] Although, as Weimann remarks, these choric characters vary "with respect to social class, psychology, and length or importance of role," most present a masculine persona:

> Launce, Speed, most of the other Shakespearean clowns, the porters in *Macbeth* and *Henry VIII*, the gravediggers in *Hamlet*, Bottom in *A Midsummer Night's Dream*, the nurse in *Romeo and Juliet*, Richard Gloucester, Iago, the Fool, and partly, Edmund in King Lear, Falstaff, Thersites, Apemantus, and – with some reservations – Aaron in *Titus Andronicus*, the Bastard Falconbridge in *King John*, and Autolycus in *The Winter's Tale*. Also belonging to this group are characters whose status within court groupings is temporarily changed or weakened as a result of real or feigned madness (Edgar, Lear, Hamlet, and, to a lesser extent, Ophelia). Taken together, these characters can be identified with a stage position that functions to greater and lesser degrees . . . as a means of achieving a special role and meaning within the play. (224–5)

The only women in this company of clownish commentators are the Nurse and "to a lesser extent," Ophelia. Although the list is, as Weimann acknowledges, incomplete, in one play after another, the comic counter-voice, like the subject of the reflective soliloquy, is male. From what space, then, on the Shakespearean stage, could a woman's countervoice be heard?

Playing the Clown

Clowns always speak of the same thing, they speak of hunger: hunger for food, hunger for sex, but also hunger for dignity, hunger for identity, hunger for power.

Dario Fo

Within the ancient tradition of which Fo writes, the anarchic laughter and feral gesticulation of the hungry clown sometimes, as Hamlet complains, disrupt the playwright's plot:

> And let those that play your clowns speak no more than is set down for them, for there be of them that will themselves laugh to set on some quantity of barren spectators to laugh too, though in the mean time some necessary question of the play be then to be consider'd. That's villainous, and shows a most pitiful ambition in the fool that uses it.
>
> (III. ii. 38–45)

Among critics who identify Hamlet with Shakespeare, the Prince's prefer-ence has lent the bard's authority to the *locus* over the *platea*, aristocratic narrative over plebeian commentary, word over gesture, and the author's over the actor's invention. But the players, hearing Hamlet's speech, also know that in this theatre that holds the mirror up to nature, clowning holds the mirror up to theatre. For the clown who says more than is set down for him, who improvises, who speaks to the playgoers and solicits their responses, exercises his liberty by continually risking the actor's freedom "not to be interfered with."[15]

What clowning is to theatre, femininity is to clowning. The clown may ridicule femininity with his masks and metamorphoses, but the body beneath is traditionally male.[16] Hence women who wear red noses rather than false lashes have left little record in cultural history. Mahadev L. Apte erroneously asserts that no women clowns or tricksters can be found in folk narrative (70), while John H. Towson's history of clowning names only Mathurine, jester to the French court from the reign of Henri III to that of Louis XIII (24).[17]

Women in theatre and circus have lately been casting off their feathers and false lashes to hold up a mirror in which the clown can see his own red nose. As they do, they provide methods and materials for a feminist revision of Shakespearean characterology. They suggest that there may be a great many more clowns than are dreamt of in the philosophies of Britain's royal theatres or North America's Shakespeare festivals.[18] Clowns populate the world of *Othello*, for example, a play whose debt to *commedia dell'arte* theatre historians have remarked. Each of the leading characters resembles one of *commedia*'s stock figures: Othello the foreign Capitano; Iago, the knave Brighella; Desdemona the Inamorata; and Emilia the soubrette Columbine, the Inamorata's confidante.[19]

Although the stock *commedia* characters may not be able to discharge all the duties of *Othello*'s *dramatis personae*, they can enrich the confrontation with tradition that enters the Shakespearean player's rehearsal process. This confrontation is arduous and inevitable; tradition is the source of the player's confidence. Tradition is also, as Raymond Williams observes, "an interpretation of the past: a selection and valuation of ancestors" (*Modern Tragedy*, 16). Players who acknowledge the presence of Brighella, Pantelone, and Columbine in *Othello* may discover other ancestors than those the still-pervasive naturalism of twentieth-century theatre has se-lected and valued. In the willow scene, for example, when Emilia urges Desdemona to resist monogamy and its discontents, a Stanislavskian tradi-tion will suggest that the player bring her own fugitive, clamorous, ignoble, or beguiling memories and desires to the text:

> But I do think it is their husbands' faults
> If wives do fall. Say that they slack their duties
> And pour our treasures into foreign laps;
> Or else break out in peevish jealousies,
> Throwing restraint upon us; or say they strike us,
> Or scant our former having in despite:
> Why, we have galls; and though we have some grace,
> Yet have we some revenge.
>
> (IV. iii. 86–93)

Yet in the same speech, the clown Columbine is speaking of hunger. And her advice can be directed not only to the Inamorata, but to the audience as well:

> Let husbands know
> Their wives have sense like them; they see, and smell,
> And have their palates both for sweet and sour,
> As husbands have. What is it that they do
> When they change us for others? Is it sport?
> I think it is. And doth affection breed it?
> I think it doth. Is't frailty that thus errs?
> It is so too. And have not we affections,
> Desires for sport, and frailty, as men have?
>
> (IV. iii. 93–101)

The player who incorporates Columbine's *concetti* into Emilia's commentary on marriage may occupy a *platea* where she will discover a liberating "on-stage-ness" unknown to naturalism.

This liberation serves the player better than it does the character, for of course the narrative rushes on to Desdemona's death and then Emilia's own. Although the clown traditionally survives to treat death "as a laughing matter," Emilia lacks his ancient immunity; she can neither overcome nor outlast the authority that oppresses her.[20] For Shakespeare's women, playing the clown is sometimes playing with death. Ophelia, having delivered a clownish commentary in her madness, is buried in the jester's grave.[21] And sometimes femininity lights fools the way to dusty death. The doubling of Cordelia and the Fool trembles at the extreme verge of *King Lear*'s promised horror. As Lear dwindles to Lear's shadow, Lear's Fool shadows Cordelia until "my poor fool is hanged" (V. iii. 306).

At the Shakespearean crossroads of femininity and clowning, then, there is danger of death for both clowns and women. Yet with this danger comes the opportunity to express the hungers of the female clown – hunger, like her male counterpart's, for food, for sex, for dignity, identity, and power. Hunger also for theatrical transformations that will turn fictions of femininity into roles for living women.

Such transformations may occur when clown theatre's physical characterization and Shakespeare's verbal drama unite to create an articulate body – a body for which word and gesture are one. Patricia Parker's warning to the critic therefore holds true for the player as well. To foreground the "political Shakespeare," she argues, "without taking seriously the linguistic one, is, for all its recontextualizing value . . . unnecessarily to short-circuit or foreclose the process of moving from literary text to social text" (94). In an embodied text, vowels and consonants, verbs and nouns, iambs, anapests, and trochees are blood, marrow, sinew. To foreclose the process of incorporating them is to sever not only text from performance, but the head from the body.

Some such injury to the corporeal register of the player's work inevitably occurs when it is translated into the cerebral discourses of criticism.[22] But to restore at least its metrical and syntactic elements, I turn to Joan of Arc, then to Cressida, and finally to the Jailer's Daughter, whose anonymity I propose to alter. Following the example of Mieke Bal, who in her study of the Book of Judges named its nameless women in accord with the roles they played in their various stories, I shall call the Jailer's Daughter Filia.[23]

Joan, Cressida, and Filia come from plays of different genres, from different playhouses, and from different moments in the development of Renaissance theatre. Joan appears in an Elizabethan history play originally performed in the public playhouse where medieval theatrical traditions were most resilient; Cressida in a play of problematic genre and venue that dates from the middle of Shakespeare's career; and Filia in a Jacobean romance, written collaboratively and played at the elite indoor theatre of Blackfriars. Each has been disparaged in critical and theatrical tradition but each has at least momentary access to the *platea*. Each has occasion to express the hungers of the clown.

Devil or devil's dam

O hold me not with silence overlong.
1 Henry VI, V. iii. 16

From the perspective of the French Dauphin, Joan is "Astrea's daughter" (I. vi); in Talbot's English eyes, she is either "devil or devil's dam" (I. v). The contradiction is apparently resolved in favor of the English, when, during the last battle scene, Joan invokes supernatural aid. The demons that then appear have led numerous critics and directors to conclude, with Talbot, that they knew this all along: Joan is a sorceress and a strumpet. Ocular proof of her demonic sexuality retroactively grants Talbot the right to interpret Joan as Ulysses interprets Cressida.

Feminist critics of *1 Henry VI* have doubted this right, observing that both the French and English views are validated theatrically during the course of Joan's seven scenes. She is first a numinous presence whose powers of divination are revealed on stage. She is then a shrewdly pragmatic military leader, and those skills too are represented. Finally, she is a witch, resorting ignominiously to feminine evasions and deceptions, enduring sexual humiliations.[24] These discontinuous images suit a script in which all the *dramatis personae* are emphatically *personae* rather than persons. They insist that the player work through mask and gesture rather than motive and emotion.[25]

There is another fissure in Joan's characterization. In Act IV, Joan stands over Talbot's corpse, ridiculing the rhetorical bravado of the heroics played out on the *locus*:

> Here's a silly stately style indeed!
> The Turk, that two and fifty kingdoms hath,
> Writes not so tedious a style as this.
> Him that thou magnifi'st with all these titles
> Stinking and fly-blown lies here at our feet.
>   (IV. vii. 72–6)

In this scene, the clown who treats death as a laughing matter speaks from the fictive body of a female character. The conjuration scene of the last act, however, denies Joan the clown's triumphant resilience.

She enters alone and begins with one expository line in direct address: "The Regent conquers, and the Frenchmen fly" (V. iii. 1). Her soliloquy then modulates into apostrophe:

> Now help, ye charming spells and periapts,
> And ye choice spirits that admonish me
> And give me signs of future accidents.   (*Thunder.*)
> You speedy helpers, that are substitutes
> Under the lordly Monarch of the North,
> Appear, and aid me in this enterprise.
>   (*Enter* FIENDS.)

When the fiends appear (as Quarto and Folio stage directions indicate), she speaks to her onstage audience:

> This speedy and quick appearance argues proof
> Of your accustom'd diligence to me.
> Now, ye familiar spirits, that are cull'd
> Out of the powerful regions under earth,
> Help me this once, that France may get the field.
> *(They walk, and speak not.)*
> O, hold me not with silence over-long!
> Where I was wont to feed you with my blood,
> I'll lop a member off and give it you
> In earnest of a further benefit,
> So you do condescend to help me now.
> *(They hang their heads.)*
> No hope to have redress? My body shall
> Pay recompense, if you will grant my suit.
> *(They shake their heads.)*
> Cannot my body nor blood-sacrifice
> Entreat you to your wonted furtherance?
> Then take my soul – my body, soul, and all,
> Before that England give the French the foil.
> *(They depart.)*

As they depart, the speech modulates again, paralleling its opening structure in a half line of direct address followed by a choric prophecy:

> See, they forsake me! Now the time is come
> That France must vail her lofty-plumed crest
> And let her head fall into England's lap.
> My ancient incantations are too weak,
> And hell too strong for me to buckle with:
> Now, France, thy glory droopeth to the dust.
> (V. iii. 2–29)

The prosodic texture of the speech harmonizes with the rhetorical formality of the trilogy and its emblematic characterology. There are few enjambed lines, and the caesurae often coincide with syntactical breaks. The insistent iambic pulse admits only one metrical substitution in twenty-nine lines: an anapest quickens the pace upon the devils' entrance.

The clown's heteroglossia of ragged rhymes, puns, and proverbs finds no place here. Yet within the range of the play's rhetorical strategies, tensions between the repetitive structure of the iambic line and the heterogeneity of the diction emerge. An interweaving of monosyllables and polysyllables keeps the caesura in motion; it also keeps words crossing the boundaries of the individual feet: "Now, ye/ fami/ liar spir/ its, that/ are cull'd / Out of/ the power/ ful re/ gions un/ der earth." "High terms" suitable for military and diplomatic exploits – enterprise, earnest, benefit, redress, recompence, furtherance – are weighted with earth, blood (twice), body (twice), and dust. The heterogeneous diction underscores the liminality of a speaker who crosses boundaries between the aggrandized actions of aristocrats and the unstoried lives of peasants. The player who grasps the subtle traversings of the poetic line also grasps the textual foundation of the liminality that had enabled Joan to play the clown over Talbot's corpse.

The verbs lend the player energy to expedite her movement from war through sorcery to the stake. Many are imperative, others are present or future indicative, and almost all are monosyllabic: fly, help, give, aid, cull, help (again), get, hold, feed, lop, pay, take, give (again), vail, fall, droop. The remaining polysyllabic verbs are similarly strenuous: conquer, admonish, appear, argue, condescend, entreat, forsake, and buckle. Such verbs animate the textual body of the speech. At first, they invite the player to assert her theatrical presence in exhortation. While the demons "speak not," "hang their heads," and "shake their heads," their lethargy creates an increasing tension that can impel the player to greater exertions: the energy of the scene is still hers. When at last "They depart," that tension is lost and with it, the theatrical vitality of the *mise en scène*: France's, and Joan's, glory droops in the dust.

This poetic closure records an innovative *coup de théâtre*. The authorial hand that had allowed a female character to invade the traditionally masculine *platea* now banishes her. Joan's lackadaisical fiends (whose enfeeblement the stage directions explicitly demand) are descended from the exuberant tricksters who had been residents of the *platea* from the moralities through *Doctor Faustus*. Clowns and devils, Michael Bristol remarks, share a theatrical vocabulary of "firecrackers, thrashing, horns, animal masks, [and] drenchings" (154–5). But on the *platea* occupied by Joan of Arc, this rough magic fails. Unlike the devils of *Doctor Faustus*, Joan's spirits are denied their ancient rights of mockery. Holding Joan in silence overlong, the dispirited devils abandon her to the justice of the *locus*. At the close, an ineluctable femininity hinders the vocations of both warrior and clown.

A life in rhyme

> Who shall be true to us,
> When we are so unsecret to ourselves?
> *Troilus and Cressida*, III. ii. 124–5

When, in her final scene, Joan "squirms away from the stake that awaits her," she resembles Cressida, Michael Hattaway suggests, "a woman alone, prey to the sexual violence of enemy soldiers" (27). But while Joan's invocation iterates the formal rhetoric of *1 Henry VI*, Cressida's rhymed soliloquies complicate the verbal texture of a play in which rhyme is rare.[26] The "armed Prologue" presents the play in orotund blank verse; Troilus has three blank verse soliloquies; Thersites addresses the audience three times in prose; and Pandarus offers an epilogue that begins in prose, turns to a lyric of two pentameter couplets, and then, after a hexameter line that sets the conclusion off from the song, ends with rhymed couplets. Lovers and clowns both enjoy the privileges of soliloquy, but with a nice attention to linguistic difference. Troilus's blank verse and Thersites' prose meet the expectations of the critical commonplace that distinguishes between the diction of high and low characters, and the epilogue embraces its lyric conventions. But why does Cressida speak in rhyme?[27]

In Act I, Cressida addresses the audience on the subject of the ephemeral nature of male desire:

> Words, vows, gifts, tears, and love's full sacrifice,
> He offers in another's enterprise,
> But more in Troilus thousandfold I see
> Than in the glass of Pandar's praise may be;
> Yet hold I off. Women are angels, wooing:
> Things won are done, joy's soul lies in the doing.
> That she belov'd knows nought that knows not this:
> Men prize the thing ungain'd more than it is.
> That she was never yet that ever knew
> Love got so sweet as when desire did sue.
> Therefore this maxim out of love I teach:
> Achievement is command; ungain'd, beseech.
> (I. ii. 282–93)

These rhymed couplets charge the player with different tasks than would blank verse. They offer, and withhold, different pleasures.

Despite the complexity of the argument, the thought is contained within the individual couplets, for only two lines are enjambed (see–be and knew–sue). The medial caesurae are often strongly marked, especially at the center of the speech, as it moves from personal revelation ("Yet hold I off") to universal significance ("Women are angels"), or, in Williams's taxonomy, from the reflexive to the generic. The coincidence of line and syntax, the weight of the caesurae and especially the repetitive force of rhyme can all encourage the interactive address of the *platea*, with its privilege of social commentary.

Yet at last, Cressida's rhymes, like Joan's fiends, confine her to the *locus*. The end-stopped lines emphasize what Cicely Berry calls the story the last words tell (181–2): sacrifice–enterprise, see–be, wooing–doing, this–is, knew–sue, teach–beseech. In this text of eroticized violence and belligerent eroticism, the story of the last words is one in which the repetitiveness of rhyme insists on the inevitability of harm. Action is here performed at the expense of the performer and knowledge gained at the knower's cost. The rhymes deflect the speaker from action, for their gravitational pull toward the ends of the lines combines with a curious lassitude of the verbs. The speaker is the active subject of only three verbs. Where the verbal energy of Joan's speech drives the player forward, Cressida speaks in a passive voice: "things won are done." Even the active voice circumscribes itself, contradicting the speaker's capacity for intervention: in the line "Women are angels, wooing" an implied subject of "wooing," "men," is more active than the actual subject of the sentence, "women." The subject is similarly traversed in the line "That she was never yet that ever knew." In the phrase "Yet hold I off," the inversion of subject and verb, the weight of monosyllables, the relatively weak stress on the pronoun all underscore the negation of activity. Finally, even this tenuous relation between speaking subject and verb breaks down. Cressida disappears into the gnomic ellipses of the closing line: "Achievement is command, ungain'd, beseech."

Cressida's vulnerability is so deeply etched into her language that it entraps and at last engulfs the speaker. Her rhymes become a mimetic representation of the alienated coquetry that Ulysses attributes to Cressida; her aphorisms evoke the anti-feminism of popular wisdom, ironically anticipating the proverbs that animate the lovers' exchange of vows: "Yea, let them say, to stick the heart of falsehood. / 'As false as Cressid'" (III. ii. 195–86). The structure of the soliloquy enables and even encourages the player to provide an eroticized aesthetic pleasure by playing Cressida in the posture of a whore.

Cressida's second and final soliloquy again turns rhymed couplets and aphorism against the speaker:

> Troilus, farewell! One eye yet looks on thee.
> But with my heart the other eye doth see.
> Ah, poor our sex! This fault in us I find,
> The error of our eyes directs our minds.
> What error leads must err; O then conclude,
> Minds swayed by eyes are full of turpitude.
>
> (V. ii. 107–12)

This soliloquy, like Cressida's earlier one, operates on what Williams calls the border between the reflexive and the generic, as the speaker turns from a personal crisis to articulate a common condition. The common condition here is specifically female and the speaker's self-loathing a pretext for misogyny. The formal repetition of rhymed couplets implies a continuity of character that belies Troilus's coarse interpretation of the scene: "This is, and is not, Cressid" (V. ii. 146). Cressida is constant indeed: her reiterated rhyme renews and deepens the alienation of the "Women are angels" soliloquy. It underscores Cressida's collusion with the closing couplet of Thersites' commentary: "A proof of strength she could not publish more, / Unless she said, 'My mind is now turn'd whore'" (V. ii. 113–14).

Cressida's soliloquies promise her the privileges of the countervoice and then mock her with a rhetorical agenda for quiescence. She is shadowed in ellipses, bound with rhyme, and haunted by the misogyny of both popular lore and learned tradition. She speaks less as a clownish commentator than as a ventriloquist's dummy. Neither the presentational nor representational elements of her speeches encourage her to tell her own history of masculine oppression rather than Troilus's tale of feminine treachery: naturalism may founder on the artificiality of the rhyme, while a gestic style must overcome the obscurity of the syntax. Cressida's life in rhyme diminishes the sympathy due to interiority without enabling the player to comment on interiority's illusions.

Filia comes to a feminine ending

Some wenches,
Some honest-hearted maids, will sing my dirge.
The Two Noble Kinsmen, II. vi. 14–15

Despite Cressida's marginality, first as the daughter of a traitor and then as a captive in the Greek camp, both rank and gender bind her to the *locus*. Filia, like Joan, is a plebeian character who embodies the clown's resistance to social regulation without enjoying his resilience, for the narrative demands Filia's social and sexual humiliation. But the player's fate is happier. In her four soliloquies, she spends more time alone on stage than most of Shakespeare's women, and much of that time is spent *with* the audience, for the rhetorical devices of her speeches, especially in the first two, encourage interaction.[28]

The first, in Act II, scene iv, opens with an analysis of the barriers she faces in her quest for Palamon's love:

Why should I love this gentleman? 'Tis odds
He never will affect me; I am base,
My father the mean keeper of his prison,
And he a prince. To marry him is hopeless;
To be his whore is witless. Out upon't!
What pushes are we wenches driven to
When fifteen once has found us!
(II. iv. 1–7)

As this exploration modulates into narrative, she confides in the audience: "Once he kiss'd me – / I lov'd my lips the better ten days after" (25–6). She concludes the soliloquy, as she began, with direct questions:

What should I do to make him know I love him?
For I would fain enjoy him. Say I ventur'd
To set him free? what says the law then?
Thus much for law or kindred! I will do it,
And this night, or to-morrow, he shall love me.
(II. iv. 29–33)

This is, as Paul Bertram remarks, a distinctive voice: "she exclaims, she questions, she narrates, she speculates, she rapsodizes, she is by sudden turns thoughtful, impudent, wistful, exuberant, matter-of-fact" (225).

Filia's speech does not resemble the clown's traditional heteroglossia, which had no place in the elite private playhouses. Yet during this soliloquy she occupies a position analogous to the *platea* of the popular stage. She solicits strong and even active responses from the audience. Her exclamations, questions, narratives, speculations, and rapsodies create a feminine countervoice that is authorized to gain the spectators' approval for the *mésalliance* of plebeian and patrician. Eschewing the boisterous puns and proverbs of popular tradition, this feminine countervoice of the private playhouse is characterized especially by the Fletcherian poetic device of feminine endings, a final unstressed syllable on which fully half the lines of Filia's first and second soliloquies end.[29]

Feminine endings, as George Wright notes, give almost as much stress to a line's conclusion as rhyme. But unlike rhyme, they subvert the straightforward progress of the pentameter line, for they pursue the process of a thought that may not come to a tidy and emphatic conclusion:

Whether the choice of the term *feminine* to describe this ending was accidental or fitted contemporary notions of gender, iambic verse that regularly ends with an unstressed syllable takes on a quality which, in different lines, may be variously described as soft, haunting, yearning, pliant, seductive. In verse that is enjambed, it helps to threaten our sense of the line as a line, as pentameter; in endstopped verse, it subtly undermines the line's iambic (or masculine) character. (164)

The feminine endings of Filia's soliloquies, then, originate in the iambic pentamenter line that is, as Belsey argues, the prosodic precondition of interiority. At the same time, they transgress it. The player who recognizes Filia's metrical excess may ground her character's lawless desires in thought that is not quite subdued to the linguistic form it works in.

The second soliloquy takes place after she has freed Palamon and sent him, still in chains, to a nearby wood to hide until she comes to bring him files and food. She begins with a cry of triumph:

> Let all the Dukes and all the devils roar,
> He is at liberty! I have ventur'd for him.
> (II. vi. 1–2)

The story of this venture reestablishes the confidential mood of the earlier soliloquy:

> If the law
> Find me, and then condemn me for't, some wenches,
> Some honest-hearted maids, will sing my dirge,
> And tell to memory my death was noble,
> Dying almost a martyr.
>
> (II. vi. 13–17)

Feminine endings, narrative, speculation, and exclamation remain. But the rhetorical questions that encouraged interaction have disappeared. The audience begins to recede before a fictive cortège of rebellious women, as Filia invokes a community of "honest-hearted maids" who create their own unofficial myths and rituals of sexuality, death, and mourning.

In the third soliloquy, her anecdotes become fantasies and her rhetorical questions are introverted:

> Dissolve, my life, let not my sense unsettle
> Lest I should drown, or stab, or hang myself.
> O state of nature, fail together in me,
> Since thy best props are warp'd! So which way now?
> The best way is the next way to a grave;
> Each errant step beside is torment. Lo
> The moon is down, the crickets chirp, and screech-owl
> Calls in the dawn! All offices are done
> Save what I fail in. But the point is this —
> An end, and that is all.
>
> (III. ii. 29–38)

This speech drives Filia toward another feminine ending, a madness that, as Wright observes of the poetic device, "may be variously described as soft, haunting, yearning, pliant, seductive." It will, by the conclusion of Act III, confine her almost entirely to the *locus*. Her social commentary in her last soliloquy, like Ophelia's, lies less in the arguments she presents than in the example she inadvertently sets:

> I am very cold, and all the stars are out too,
> The little stars and all, that look like aglets.
> The sun has seen my folly. Palamon!
> Alas, no; he's in heaven. Where am I now?

Yonder's the sea, and there's a ship. How't tumbles!
And there's a rock lies watching under water;
Now, now, it beats upon it – now, now, now!
There's a leak sprung, a sound one. How they cry!
[Open] her before the wind! you'll lose all else.
Up with a course or two, and tack about, boys.

(III. iv. 1–10)

Even here, Filia's vision of shipwreck, with its exclamations and its reiterated "now, now, now," allows the player to choose physical actions that can command the stage. The conclusion of the speech also recalls the energetic eroticism of Filia's earlier speeches: "O for a prick now, like a nightingale / To put my breast against! I shall sleep like a top else" (III. iv. 25–6). But she no longer enjoys the intimacy with the audience that she had established in the first, presentational soliloquies. As she withdraws, the femininized clown begins to merge with the medicalized madwoman.[30] Filia's hysteria completes a Shakespearean progression from the residual *platea* and *locus* toward the emerging proscenium stage on which women will be playing these roles originally scripted for boys.

My search for the presentational countervoice in Joan's, Cressida's, and Filia's soliloquies is of course subjective, provisional, and always renegotiable in the collaborative enterprise of rehearsal and performance. Joan's energetic verbs and Filia's feminine endings seem to me more immediately amenable to a feminist practice than Cressida's rhymes, but other interpreters, or I myself on other occasions, may encounter different problems and discover different solutions. For these examples of the sexual politics of the prosody, syntax, and diction are not proofs that Shakespeare is or is not a "patriarchal bard." The politics of prosody will not corroborate such categorical pronouncements, though it may enable a player to avoid embodying a more misogynistic text than the bard has authorized.[31] Nor will it transform the politics of casting, staging, costume or lighting design in the contemporary director's and designer's theatre. So I turn now to the records of that theatre, to ask what acts of resistance Joan, Cressida, and Filia have performed there.

Playing the Boy's Part

It takes an artist nowadays to shock people.
Brecht, *The Threepenny Opera*

The theatrical practices through which Shakespeare has been produced and reproduced span a continuum from the improvisatory interaction between the player and the playgoer on the Elizabethan *platea*, to the Restoration amalgam of a non-illusionistic forestage with the voyeurist blandishments of perspective scenery, to the Victorian tableaux where waterfalls bubbled and rabbits scampered behind proscenium arches, to the impenetrable fourth wall of cinema and video. In contemporary Britain and North America, the conventions for choosing a spot on that continuum originated in what J. L. Styan has named "the Shakespeare revolution," during which Shakespearean staging moved "from the elaborate decoration of Beerbohm Tree to the austerities of Peter Hall, from the illusory realism of Henry Irving to the non-illusory statements of Peter Brook" (1).

The latter stages of "the Shakespeare revolution" enlisted Brecht's gestic theatre in the enterprise of consolidating the revolt against nineteenth-century illusionism.[32] Although Brecht has, in the West, had an apolitical aesthetic thrust upon him, he may thus be credited with reviving some of the populist exuberance of the Shakespearean *platea*. And for many materialist critics, his doctrine that modern productions of the Elizabethans must "play these old works historically" (*Messingkauf Dialogues*, 63) still holds out the promise of a political Shakespeare, the ally of radical rather than reactionary theatre.

To exemplify the virtues of this gestic Shakespeare, they point to Jane Howell's videotape of the first tetralogy for the BBC Shakespeare. In emphasizing the episodic structure of the play text over illusionistic design and in retrieving its rhetorical characterology through ensemble playing, Howell discovered analogies between the means of television production and those of the Shakespearean playhouse. Thus, several critics observe, she achieved Brecht's goal of "playing the old works historically." For Graham Holderness, her "production techniques . . . deliver those theatrical energies inscribed into the texts by the conditions of their original performance," provoking "from them their residual latent content of popular experience" (186).[33]

The hope that Brecht will redeem the political pledges of Shakespearean scripts is less compelling from the perspective of a feminist player.[34] Restoring the "latent content of popular experience" will not in itself improve the lot of Shakespeare's women on or off stage. Howell's *1 Henry VI*, however, did evade the sexism that has often been gratuitously introduced into other interpretations of the play. Because the first tetralogy identifies Englishness with masculinity, a gestic presentation that exposes the puerile greed of the squabbling aristocracy also reveals the relation of patriotism and patriarchy. Each of the women's roles in *1 Henry VI* – Joan, the Countess of Auvergne and Margaret – link femininity and France, misogyny and xenophobia. These structural symmetries define "the conflict between England and France as a conflict between masculine and feminine values – chivalric virtue vs pragmatic craft, historical fame vs physical reality, patriarchal age vs subversive youth, high social rank vs low, self vs other" (Rackin, 332). Brechtian strategies that undermine jingoism therefore also undermine sexism; to resist Talbot's heroics is to enlist on Joan's side.

Unlike many directors, Howell did not equate the perspective of the male characters with authorial instructions. In her version, Talbot's misogynist commentary is merely the unvalidated rant of a character who is, as Dennis Bingham remarks, "self-consciously macho" (224). The question masculinist interpretation asks, whether Joan is a saint or a strumpet, does not arise during a performance from which the director has silently deleted the customary privilege accorded to misogyny's spokesmen.[35]

Such revivals of presentational playing do not inevitably challenge the historical forms of misogyny that naturalism has made habitual. In *Playing Shakespeare*, a television series and subsequently a book that offers demonstrations of John Barton's work with members of the Royal Shakespeare Company, the director describes the poetic and rhetorical strategies of the play text as "stage direction in shorthand": "A short verse line suggests a pause, and a shared line says 'pick up the cue'" (32). The stage directions for soliloquies, he argues, usually forbid the public solitude of illusionistic theatre (94). Directing Jane Lapotaire in Cressida's first soliloquy, Barton suggests that the "versified stage directions" of the soliloquy demand "sharing with the audience" rather than enclosing the character within an interior monologue. For Barton, this is, as William Worthen observes, an ideologically neutral aesthetic choice (450). Yet such "sharing" does not mitigate misogyny, for what Barton wants Lapotaire to share is Cressida's "vanity and her self-absorption": "Show off and flaunt to [the audience]. Show them how clever you are" (95). Barton directs Lapotaire to replay his 1968 production, when Francesca Annis's Cressida entered the Greek camp costumed as a courtesan.[36]

Other directors and players have challenged this interpretation. In the same year as Barton's production, Joseph Papp, directing the play for the

New York Shakespeare Festival, described the scene in the Greek camp as "a kind of rape scene," arguing that Cressida's victimization begins with Troilus's callow reaction to her exile: "How my achievements mock me" (IV. ii. 69). In Howard Davies's 1985 production for the Royal Shakespeare Company, Juliet Stevenson's Cressida emerged as a woman "trying to protect herself in a world where there was no faith, no morality" (Woddis, 15). David William's 1987 Stratford Festival production, indebted to Davies and Stevenson, also exposed Cressida's victimization. In the eavesdropping scene, during which the audience sees Thersites watch Troilus and Ulysses spy on Diomedes and Cressida, Diomedes subjected Peggy Coffey's Cressida to harrowing symbolic violence, intermittently underscored by physical menace. He left her so near hysteria that when she came to her soliloquy, the words were virtually unintelligible, The text of Cressida's collusion gave way before an image which represented the terror of rape as forcefully as Gloucester's onstage blinding represents the horror of mutilation.

While Coffey's inarticulate hysteria erased the image of the coquette, it also demonstrated the difficulty of escaping from the *locus*. Cressida stood upstage, with Ulysses and Troilus downstage left and Thersites right. Thus framed, even choices that redeem Cressida from coquetry work to her destruction; only by demonstrating victimization does she refute the charge of promiscuity. Barbara Bowen, discussing Stevenson's Cressida, asks whether such a "proto-feminist forced into a pose of submission" really differs from the sanatized heroine in Dryden's revision of the play, "who has no way to prove her chastity but to kill herself?" (285). The sympathy that some directors and players now grant to the character is rooted in the same dichotomy of martyr and slut that had previously condemned her.

Troilus's response to the scene, however, in some measure completed Cressida's gest. His self-indulgent grieving for what he so willfully interpreted as Cressida's faithlessness went extravagantly over the top. The audience had just seen a rape scene; they now saw patriarchal ideology at work as Troilus bustled about blaming the victim: "The fractions of her faith, orts of her love, / The fragments, scraps, the bits and greasy relics / Of her o'er-eaten faith, are given to Diomed" (V. ii. 158–60). Such moments can move at least some of the spectators from empathy to anger. Yet the program notes directed the spectators to deny the violence that they witnessed: "No sooner has Troilus won Cressida than they are parted and, despite her desperate protests, she is sent to join her father in the Greek camp. There, confused and susceptible in her new womanhood, she is quickly seduced by Diomedes" (n.p.).

A contradiction between program notes and performance choices also characterized Barry Kyle's 1986 production of *The Two Noble Kinsmen* for the Royal Shakespeare Company. The plot degrades Filia, as *Troilus and Cressida* degrades Cressida, and it is this aspect of her role that Simon Trussler's program notes emphasize. The Jailer's Daughter is one of Shakespeare's "wanton wenches from the lower orders who give rein to their sexual appetites." She is "contrasted with high-born ladies who put a proper price on their own virginity," Trussler remarks, "less a mad sister to Ophelia than a tragi-comic version of the all-too available Jaquenetta in *Love's Labour's Lost* – or perhaps a sort of siamese twin from *As You Like It*, combining the honest earthiness of Audrey with the pretensions of poor Phebe, likewise fobbed-off with an inferior substitute for daring to fall in love beyond her social station" (xvii).[37]

Like the Ontario production of *Troilus and Cressida*, the Royal Shakespeare Company production of *The Two Noble Kinsmen* complicated the sexism and elitism that the commentary attributed to the play text, for the Jailer's Daughter was socially marginal while Imogen Stubbs, who played her, was theatrically central.[38] Her wit and resilience granted dignity to the character's erotic energy and her vulnerability made that dignity poignant. She became, however, more a mad sister to Ophelia and less like Phoebe or Audrey than Trussler's remarks had anticipated. Stubbs generated a sympathy for Filia that middle-class theatregoers of the late twentieth century happily extend to the romantic figures of the *locus*. She achieved her triumph at some cost to the rebelliousness that drives Filia onto the *platea* to speak her mutinous mind.

But like the gestic moment that emerged from the conjunction of Diomedes' brutality, Cressida's hysteria and Troilus's narcissism in the Stratford Festival production, Stubbs's performance carried Filia back toward an expression of the clown's hungers. Her athletic skills enabled her, during her mad scenes, to climb a flagpole and to cross downstage walking on her hands while singing. Such technical prowess, used for such explicitly theatrical actions, charges the nexus of performer and character with an extraordinary vitality. It insists that a character in a play is, in

Michael Goldman's phrase, "something an actor *does*" (*Acting and Action*, 149). When Filia became something that Imogen Stubbs did, the performer's skill and strength turned the character's madness not, like Ophelia's, to prettiness, but to power.

In various degrees and with various qualifications these productions of *1 Henry VI*, *Troilus and Cressida*, and *The Two Noble Kinsmen* each offer techniques that can move feminist critique toward new theatrical practices. The player may, like Imogen Stubbs, command special, empowering skills; she may, as Stevenson and Coffey do, revise the performance choices, tasks, and motivations that have trivialized or demonized female characters; she may, like Howell's ensemble, deny misogyny's spokesmen their customary authorization.

Yet I have not described feminist productions but rather offered a feminist's description of productions that took place in venues whose prestige commands the attention of critics and practitioners. Such venues, however, offer neither the only nor the most likely material conditions for a feminist Shakespeare. Ranging from the endowed monuments of national theatres through amateur workshops in basements and storefronts, contemporary theatrical cultures trace their descent variously to Stanislavski, Brecht, and Artaud; they respond to a history of actresses, proscenium stages, and bardolotry; and they now confront the social and political conflicts of postmodernity, whether eagerly or gingerly, wittily or sluggishly. To mobilize this theatrical eclecticism for a feminist Shakespeare, I turn from soloists to choruses and from established players to an anonymous ensemble, seeking other entrances to a Shakespearean stage on which a woman may play the clown.

The Theatricality of Witchcraft

To any unprejudiced reader – which would seem to exclude Shakespeare himself, his contemporary audiences and almost all literary critics – it is surely clear that positive value in *Macbeth* lies with the three witches. The witches are the heroines of the piece, however little the play itself recognizes the fact, and however much the critics may have set out to defame them . . . As the most fertile force in the play, the witches inhabit an anarchic, richly ambiguous zone both in and out of official society: they live in their own world but intersect with Macbeth's. They are poets, prophetesses and devotees of female cult, radical separatists who scorn male power and lay bare the hollow sound and fury at its heart. Their words and bodies mock rigorous boundaries and make sport of fixed positions, unhinging received meanings as they dance, dissolve and re-materialize.

Terry Eagleton, *William Shakespeare*

Insisting upon textual contradictions and omissions, Eagleton dismantles the traditional image of *Macbeth*'s witches to argue that they can embody creativity rather than chaos, community rather than conspiracy. I want now to explore techniques that may realize their liminal counter-culture theatrically. This enterprise poses a theatrical problem that some literary critics find intractable. In "Text vs performance: the example of *Macbeth*," Harry Berger argues that performance resists such politicized reinterpretation, for the physical presence of the players inevitably reinforces "the coercive, collective, and ritualistic potentialities of theatre" (59, 53). The witches exemplify this conservative impulse of theatrical representation, for their

> visibility as characters on stage does not simply reify and trivialize the complex problematic of gender conflict which they come, under scrutiny of the text, to represent. Their embodiment conceals it. We do not see them as degraded images of the power and threat of femininity unless and until we have performed what is nowadays called a deconstructive reading of the text. (73)

Theatricality renders the witches "outlandish or even amusing"; they are reduced to their traditional function of securing "the manifest themes of the self-destruction of evil and the triumph of good" (67–8).[39]

In his anti-theatricalism, Berger fortuitously articulates the dilemma for a feminist staging of *Macbeth*. Performance, like criticism, may either reproduce or reevaluate the ideology with which a dominant culture invests a play text. But if a production is to challenge the theatrical tradition, as Eagleton challenges the critical tradition, it must move from critique to revision. Even as sophisticated an elucidation of the play's sexual politics as Janet Adelman's psychoanalytic reading would affirm a misogynist interpretation, were it taken as the conceptual foundation for performance:

> The play strikingly constructs the fantasy of subjection to maternal malevolence in two parts, in the witches and in Lady Macbeth, and then persistently identifies the two parts as one. Through this identification,

> Shakespeare in effect locates the source of his culture's fear of witchcraft in individual human history, in the infant's long dependence on female figures felt as all-powerful. (97)

Adelman's reading is not, like Berger's, explicitly anti-theatrical, but its feminism is theatrically inert. When performance links Lady Macbeth's domestic (and sometimes erotic) dominance to the witches' prophetic powers, femininity comes to seem almost universally demonic. She becomes one of the loathly ladies, while they appear more murderously manipulative. Most importantly, to stage *Macbeth* as male fantasy is to deny that women actively participate in constructing the world of the play. It reduces the women on stage (and in the audience) to the stuff upon which misogynistic dreamwork is enacted.

To move, then, toward a *Macbeth* in which the witches are something other than what Berger calls "degraded images of the power and threat of femininity," I first note that Eagleton's image of radical separatists, however tendentious, can be corroborated by quite conservative methods of textual interpretation. In his stage history, *The Masks of Macbeth*, Marvin Rosenberg remarks that the word "witch" appears only in the stage directions and the quotation of a housewife's curse: " 'Aroint thee witch!' the rump-fed ronyon cried" (I. iii. 6). In dialogue, Shakespeare's witches call one another "sister." They describe themselves as "weyward," in definition of which Rosenberg cites the *OED*: "1. Disposed to go counter to the wishes or advice of others, or to what is reasonable; wrongheaded, intractable, self-willed; forward, perverse. 2. Capriciously wilful; conforming to no fixed rule or principle of conduct; erratic" (12). Rejecting the stage directions that countermand their self-interpretation, I shall call them the Weyward Sisters while I seek ways to make them "the heroines of the piece" when the piece is performed.

I turn first to the stage tradition. I follow the Weyward Sisters from Shakespeare's Globe to the operatic revision that D'Avenant presented during the Restoration, to the comic versions of the eighteenth and nineteenth centuries, to twentieth-century adaptations such as Charles Marowitz's *A Macbeth*. Since the Weyward Sisters are contrary, wrongheaded, and capricious, their progress is naturally erratic, and I also follow them backwards to the late medieval booth stages and sideways to the improvised *lazzi* of the *commedia dell'arte*; to Brecht's songs, captions, and montage; and finally to postmodern mime and clown theatre.[40]

My production, like their cookery, is concocted from what I find about me: I search the historical record as a trunk filled with masks, props, costumes, songs, dances, and scenarios to mount a *Macbeth* that celebrates what I shall call the theatricality of witchcraft. To suit Eagleton's words and the players' gestures, I present the Weyward Sisters as a troupe of acrobats, jugglers, musicians, mimes, clowns, puppeteers, magicians, singers, and dancers. Inhabitants of the *platea*, they not only play the roles of witches, but play *with* the roles of witches.

Tragical–Comical–Historical–Pastoral–Mythical–Musical *Macbeth*

> I was a-weary of the play, but I liked hugeously the actors.
> Margary Pinchwife in *The Country Wife*

A weyward historian, I begin with a suspect document. The record of the 1611 Globe staging of *Macbeth* in Simon Forman's *Bocke of Plaies* seems to conflict directly with the evidence of the play text. Banquo's lines, commentators find, demand withered crones:

> What are these,
> So wither'd and so wild in their attire,
> That look not like th'inhabitants o' th' earth,
> And yet are on't?
> (I. iii. 39–42)

He further specifies their appearance when he addresses them:

> You seem to understand me,
> By each at once her choppy finger laying
> Upon her skinny lips: you should be women,
> And yet your beards forbid me to interpret
> That you are so.
> (I. iii. 43–7)

Forman, however, calls them "three women fairies or nymphs" (Salgado, 31), evoking the prototypes of Shakespeare's witches in Holinshed, where an illustration displays three rather young and fashionably dressed women.

Forman often draws on Holinshed more directly than Shakespeare, and his unreliable testimony cannot recover an authentically Shakespearean image for the Weyward Sisters.[41] It can, however, question critical common sense, which knows without asking what the Jacobean stage must have meant by adjectives such as "wither'd" and nouns such as "beards." For theatre history exceeds its brief if it argues that Forman saw what Banquo suggests he should have seen rather than what Forman himself describes. Did boy actors appear in illusionistic wrinkles and whiskers? Or did the playgoers' thoughts, which Shakespeare had solicited to deck the armies of *Henry V*, also robe the Weyward Sisters? Was there, in this initial staging, consonance or dissonance between text and image, actor and role, Banquo's witches and the spectators'?

The inevitably volatile relation of text and performance is especially complicated for *Macbeth*, which may have been played not only at the Globe but also for King James at Whitehall. A court performance of *Macbeth*, unlike one at an open-air amphitheatre, must confront and may exploit the tradition of the masque, with its perspective staging, elaborate scenes and machines, lavish costumes, candlelit pageantry, and combined casts of professional players and aristocratic masquers. The play text records this confrontation in its rhyming couplets, the pageant of kings, the symbolics of color and number, and mythological metamorphoses that recall the pyrotechnics of the court masque: "Stones have been known to move and trees to speak" (Lomax, 55–69; III. iv. 122).

Paradoxically, it is the Weyward Sisters, certainly the least courtly of *Macbeth*'s creatures, who speak the tetrameter couplets that are the characteristic verse form of the masque: "Double, double, toil and trouble: / Fire burn and cauldron bubble" (IV. i. 10–11, 20–1, and 35–6). The trochaic rhythm of these lines may represent the unnatural inversion of humanity's iambic pulse, as Neil Freeman suggests (vi and n. 1). Or it may artfully mirror mundane dispositions of iamb and trochee, left and right, fair and foul. Paradoxically too, it is the Weyward Sisters who enact the magical transformations that in the masque signal the victory of aristocratic virtue, for their entrances are announced by thunder and lightening and their exits accomplished, the stage directions reiterate, by vanishing.

Such speech and actions evoke the ambiguous relationship that masquing creates between the players and their patrons. For the Weyward Sisters are to the *dramatis personae* of *Macbeth* what professional players are to aristocratic masquers. Both players and courtiers take their places in the fiction of a masque. But unlike the players' parts, the masquers' theatrical roles must complement their social roles and resolve back into them during the concluding revels.[42] The players elude this resolution. The Weyward Sisters may represent not only the fictive powers of witches but the professional liminality of actors whose age, rank, and gender do not invariably predict the roles they play.

The masquelike language and pageantry of the play text underwrote D'Avenant's notoriously spectacular revival for the elite playhouse of the Restoration. Samuel Pepys describes an operatic version of *Macbeth* that was "a most excellent play in all respects, but especially in divertisement, though it be a deep tragedy; which is a strange perfection in a tragedy, it being most proper here, and suitable" (quoted in Spencer, 621). In 1708, John Downes's *Roscius Anglicanus* testified to the continued success of *Macbeth* as extravaganza: it was presented at Dorset Garden "drest in all it's Finery, as new Cloath's, new Scenes, Machines, as flyings for the Witches, with all the singing and dancing in it . . . Excellently perform'd in the nature of an Opera" (quoted in Spencer, 620). These "divertisements" have elicited scholarly shudders. Rosenberg complains that D'Avenant reduced *Macbeth* to a "balletic, operatic frill, tinselling Shakespeare's terror with prettiness" (496). Evoking a contemptible feminization of the text, Rosenberg's diction obscures the significance of the theatrical response to a new cultural construction of gender.

The feminizing "tinsel" of Restoration productions included actresses in the roles of Lady Macbeth and Lady Macduff. The novel casting of women as women may reflect not only a new illusionistic aesthetic but also an emerging biological essentialism.[43] Representing the androgyny of the Weyward Sisters, however, remained a man's job of work. Whatever songs, dances, and "flyings" the *corps de ballet* performed, the witches' lines were apparently still spoken by men throughout the Restoration and into the eighteenth century. In Betterton's 1707 production, a Mr Johnson took the role of Hecate, while Messieurs Norris, Bullock, and Bowen played the First, Second, and Third Witches (Spencer, 622; Bartholomeusz, 18).

In later eighteenth- and nineteenth-century stagings, male comedians were cast. The *St. James Chronicle* for October 1773 criticized such casting because it turned "a solemn incantation into a ridiculous farce for the entertainment of the upper gallery" (quoted in Rosenberg, 8), but it pleased those who, like Garrick's biographer Thomas Davies, found "in the witches something odd and peculiar, and approaching to what we call

humour . . . more suitable to our notions of comic than tragic action"
(quoted in Rosenberg, 8). Fanny Kemble records that in 1833 they were
still played by "three jolly-faced fellows, whom we are accustomed to laugh
at . . . in every farce . . . with (a) due proportion of petticoats . . . jocose red
faces, peaked hats, and broomsticks" (quoted in Rosenberg, 9). As long as
their oddity seemed to have in it something "more suitable to our notions
of comic than tragic action," the Weyward Sisters were played by men.

The historical moment in which these prototypical panto dames retired
completes a change in conventions for cultural representations of women.
Echoes of the earlier tradition may occasionally ring in twentieth-century
productions, as perhaps they did in Michael MacOwen's inspired casting
of a "papably versatile Hugh Griffith" as the First Witch for his
1946 Stratford production (Evans, 89). But when women are cast as the
Weyward Sisters, as they typically are in twentieth-century productions,
they often become, as Berger complains, "spiteful pedants of mum-
bojumbo . . . shrunken figures of evil as comical as they are sinister" (64).
Played for comedy when they were played by men, the Weyward Sisters are
eroticized, demonized, and only inadvertently funny now that they are
played by women. The twentieth-century actress, like the seventeenth-
century witch, is identified with the demonic, even as a failure of theatrical
nerve attests to the banality of an obsolete evil.

The effects of this identification linger on wherever the heroic mode of
Renaissance tragedy is introverted to dramatize a contemporary discourse
of masculine angst. As the tetrameter couplets of the court masque underwrote D'Avenant's spectacle, Macbeth's soliloquies authorize the modern
tragedy of an individual consciousness in which choice, error, guilt, and
sorrow are located.[44] Trevor Nunn's celebrated 1976 Royal Shakespeare
Company production with Ian McKellan and Judi Dench, exploiting the
intimacy of The Other Place to emphasize Macbeth's soliloquies, presented
a psychologized tragedy that transformed the pageant of kings into a drug-
induced fantasia and the fifth act battle into Macbeth's nightmare.[45]

In making Macbeth's mind "full of scorpions" the spectator's point of
reference, Nunn travelled part way on the path Charles Marowitz had
blazed in his radical restaging of the play, the 1971 A Macbeth. Marowitz's
Shakespearean revisions, which cut and paste the play texts, rearranging
scenes and reassigning speeches, are, as Marowitz describes them, "nothing
more nor less than a head-on confrontation with the intellectual substruc-
ture of the plays, an attempt to test or challenge, revoke or destroy the

intellectual foundation which makes a classic the formidable thing it has become" (24).

But unlike *The Shrew*, Marowitz's 1974 revision of *The Taming of the Shrew*, *A Macbeth* does not test, challenge, revoke, or destroy Shakespeare's sexual politics. Rather, Marowitz restructured the text to present Macbeth as the "victim of a witchcraft plot masterminded by Lady Macbeth (the chief witch of a coven which included the three witches), progressively destroyed by forces he could not envisage and therefore not understand" (14). Marowitz's *Macbeth*, like Adelman's, is the tragedy of a soliloquizing soldier for whom evil takes a feminine form in order to invade his consciousness most insidiously. This putatively radical revision violates the patriarchal play text only to enter a realm of misogynistic fantasy.[46]

More recent *avant garde* revisions, incorporating feminist reevaluation, have shown less hostility to Lady Macbeth. Linda Mussmann's *M.A.C.B.E.T.H.* uses fragments of Shakespeare's text for a performance piece that reinterprets the murder of Duncan from Lady Macbeth's perspective, fragmenting the narrative structure with film, slides, overhead projections, audio and musical effects.[47] In conventional productions, too, an implicit response to feminism has reshaped the relationship between the Macbeths, though not necessarily for feminist ends. In Adrian Noble's 1986 Royal Shakespeare Company production, the play became, in Carol Rutter's words, "not so much a political tragedy of multiple betrayal as a domestic drama, the destruction of a marriage" (56). In this "domestic drama," the relationship between Jonathan Pryce's Macbeth and Sinead Cusack's Lady Macbeth was subtly played; the often embarrassing scene which precedes the murder of Lady Macduff and her children was brilliantly illuminated; and when the children reappeared as the spirits in the pageant of kings, the poignance of their physicality underscored the sterility of the Macbeths' marriage. Neither witches nor soldiers nor servants were located politically. Like the psychological privacies of Nunn's production, the domestic privacies of Noble's denied the social structures of the play's sexual politics. Noble's was not a feminist but a "post-feminist" *Macbeth*, a *Macbeth* for the era of Thatcher and Reagan, in which childlessness rather than assassination became the tragic fact.

Whether focused on heroic consciousness or domestic disintegration, the twentieth-century director's theatre has obscured the tradition that I am calling the theatricality of witchcraft. Acknowledging again, with Williams, that "a tradition is not the past, but an interpretation of the past: a selection and valuation of ancestors," I turn to this tradition to select ancestors for the new "heroines of the piece." From the Jacobean theatre, I take an implicit tension between social and theatrical role-playing; from the Restoration, an explicit exploitation of music and spectacle; and from the eighteenth and nineteenth centuries, a comic deployment of the Sisters' bewildering gender. For while Jacobean masquing, Restoration spectacle, and Victorian comedy do not enact a feminist theatricality of witchcraft, they nevertheless affirm its potentiality as an alternative to the creation of a Stanislavskian hero or the destruction of a post-feminist marriage. *Macbeth*, as its stage history reveals, can elicit varied theatrical pleasures: the pleasures not only of closure and catharsis, but of physical energy, scenic spectacle, poetic exuberance, histrionically mediated memories of and desires for community and transformation. Reviving these theatrical pleasures can enable spectators not only to resist but to *enjoy* resisting the misogyny of contemporary Shakespearean performance. Although, as Pepys remarks, "it be a strange perfection in a tragedy," it is, I think, "most proper here, and suitable," that a feminist *Macbeth* transform a tragedy of machismo and maternity into a celebration of liminality, evoking from the text a quintessentially theatrical *jouissance* that radiates from the interaction of the Weyward Sisters with their roles.

This *jouissance* elicits the gestic theatricality that is a contemporary analogue to the *platea* of the Shakespearean clown, creating moments when player and role become simultaneously visible. Such moments in *Macbeth* may emerge from tension between the physical reality of the actors' bodies and the conventions of theatrical representation: "[*The witches dance, and vanish*]" (IV. i. s.d.). They may emerge from contradictions within or among the roles a character plays: "you should be women, / And yet your beards forbid me to interpret / That you are so" (I. iii. 45–7).

In seeking these gestic moments, I again want to distinguish between social and theatrical roles, between theatre and the theatricality of everyday life, between role-playing as theatrical transformation and role-playing as social subordination. In Stoppard's *Rosencranz and Guilderstern Are Dead*, the Player King tells the feckless courtiers, "We're *actors* – we're the opposite of people" (63). Although Stoppard's antithesis may too simply separate essence and role, it can also establish the explicitly theatrical purposes of playing. It can distinguish the carnivalesque androgyny of the Weyward Sisters from the confinements of Macbeth's brutally anxious masculinity and the busy, alienated femininity of Lady Macbeth. As players, the Weyward Sisters are the "opposite" of people who occupy rigid positions in the hierarchies of rank and gender. Macbeth and Lady Macbeth, like anti-theatrical pamphleteers, accept the philological equation between theatricality and hypocrisy: "look like th' innocent flower, / But be the serpent under't" (I. vii. 65–6). They therefore refuse the theatrical *jouissance* of those who "dance and vanish" and are bound unsmiling in physical and social space. The Weyward Sisters are travelling players.

The Weyward Sisters Go on Tour

> We've got songs, dances, a few battles, a few jokes.
> Theatre Workshop, *Oh, What a Lovely War*

On one side of the playing space, there is a ragged booth stage with a legend, "The Weyward Sisters." There are masks and props about, and musical instruments; there is food and drink, for the site of the booth stage is also a campsite: the Weyward Sisters are on tour. Their troupe consists of four women and a girl, a structure that recalls the early modern touring companies of four men and a boy. It replaces the threes and multiples of three that have so often reduced the Weyward Sisters to crude archetypes of essentialized femininity, Norns or Moirae or Gravesian triple goddesses. As acrobats, jugglers, musicians, mimes, puppeteers, clowns, magicians, singers, and dancers, their theatrical witchcraft, in contrast to D'Avenant's elite spectacle, emerges from the popular tradition that Peter Brook calls "the rough theatre," the theatre of

> salt, sweat, noise, smell: the theatre that's not in a theatre, the theatre on carts, on wagons, on trestles, audiences standing, drinking, sitting round tables, audiences joining in, answering back: theatre in back rooms, upstairs rooms, barns; the one-night stands, the torn sheet pinned up across the hall, the battered screen to conceal the quick changes. (65)

This rough Shakespearean theatre reestablishes the *platea*. The theatricality of the Weyward Sisters, however, not only restores the political uses of the *platea* to the Shakespearean clown, but extends it to female characters whose clowning has hitherto been unacknowledged.

Like the travelling players of the *commedia dell'arte*, the Weyward Sisters improvise from scenarios, intercalating into them the comic routines called *lazzi*. Mel Gordon's collection of traditional *lazzi* includes several titles strangely suitable for *Macbeth*: "the *lazzo* of nightfall" "the *lazzo* of being brained," and "the *lazzo* of knocking on the door." Others emerge from the Shakespearean text. Here, the Weyward Sisters rehearse the *lazzo* of the cauldron under Hecate's direction:

> O, well done! I commend your pains,
> And every one shall share i' th' gains.
> And now about the cauldron sing,
> Like elves and fairies in a ring,
> Enchanting all that you put in.
>
> (IV. i. 39–43)

Unlike the scripted jokes of parodic subplots, improvisational *lazzi* cannot easily be subordinated to the tragic or romantic actions of the *locus*, for they privilege the player's invention. To restore improvisation to Shakespearean staging is to revive a historical moment in which the playwright shared authority with the player.

In a Shakespearean theatre that negotiates between script and improvisation, the playwright shares authority not only with the player but with the playgoer. Whenever the Weyward Sisters are not on stage, they move among and speak with the playgoers, eating, laughing, playing with them. They are neither grotesque nor glamorous. They wear rehearsal skirts and blouses in brilliant colors – reds, yellows, blues, and greens. Like the double-cast players of Brook's *A Midsummer Night's Dream*, who put on their fairy robes over their court costumes in view of the audience, the Weyward Sisters put on their witch costumes, their masks and false beards, when they perform tragedy:

> Show his eyes, and grieve his heart;
> Come like shadows, so depart.
>
> (IV. i. 110–11)

Or comedy:

> Come sisters, cheer we up his sprites,
> And show the best of our delights,

> I'll charm the air to give a sound,
> While you perform your antic round.
>
> (IV. i. 127–30)

Clowns, magicians, and acrobats, they do not create the tragic violence of the play, but, like the singer whose highland lament Joan Littlewood intercalated into her *Macbeth*, they can respond to it.[48]

At the other side of the playing space is the Macbeths' castle, which also takes its shape from a late medieval stage property: the Hellmouth. The costumes of the characters who inhabit the castle are fashionable, well-tailored garments of grey, brown, black, olive, and royal blue, with bits of metallic colors – gold, silver, brass, copper. Each character wears the same costume throughout the performance. None establishes direct contact with the audience.[49]

No sketch or scenario can anticipate the risks a fully realized production may run or the discoveries it may make. The theatricality of witchcraft, like the tragedy of the soliloquizing soldier, finally depends on the physical settings and social contexts in which the play is performed. For a radical theatre cannot remain radical in a venue dedicated to the preservation of the *status quo*. In *A Good Night Out*, John McGrath quotes Franca Rame, who, along with Dario Fo, left their popular television program to perform in workers' clubs: "This bourgeoisie did not mind our criticism, no matter how pitiless it had become [as long as] the exposure of their 'vices' occurred exclusively within the structures they controlled . . . We had to place ourselves at the service of the exploited, become their minstrels" (35).

I seek a more heterogeneous audience than Rame's for this imaginary *Macbeth*, but I heed her caveat. In the commercial or subsidized theatre, a radical vision quickly dwindles into a production concept. Macbeth's venues will always uphold Macbeth's centrality. This production, then, takes place at the instigation of the Weyward Sisters:

1. When shall we three meet again?
   In thunder, lightening, or in rain?
2. When the hurly-burly's done,
   When the battle's lost and won.
3. That will be ere the set of sun.
1. Where the place?
2.   Upon the heath.

(I. i. 1–6)

If not actually "upon the heath," then it will be performed (to quote Brook again) "in the theatre that's not a theatre," in the open air of a park or vacant lot; or in a warehouse, a storefront, any rough and ready space where there are crowds rather than audiences.

The production I have described takes its script from Shakespeare and its settings from ancient traditions of popular theatre. It draws on Brechtian strategies of representation without aiming to reproduce them; it responds to the eclectic allusiveness if not the technological sophistication of postmodern performance. But it is not an *avant garde* appropriation that severs itself from text and tradition, forcibly wresting a kernel of relevance from the disposable hull of the antique. The Weyward Sisters occupy the *platea* on behalf of Shakespeare's women *and* of Shakespeare's theatre.

Even so, those who are accustomed to seeing Shakespeare's play through the eyes of the soliloquizing soldier may not find here a recognizable *Macbeth*. For these playgoers (who, like the anti-theatrical Macbeths, do not seem to have much fun), this production may be called *Another Macbeth*, as Marowitz's revision is *A Macbeth*. Or it may be an entirely new play, requiring a new title: *The Weyward Sisters Go on Tour*.

Notes

I am grateful to Phyllis Gorfain, Barbara Hodgdon, Jean Peterson, and Debora Shuger for comments on earlier versions of this chapter and for conversations that have contributed to it.

Although I would otherwise use the term "actor" to include men and women, my argument here requires both gendered and generic terms, and so I shall in general use "actor" for men, "actress" for women, and "player" when I intend to include both.

1   Among the early feminist studies are Adelman, "This is and is not Cressid," Greene, and Yoder. For stage history and production critique, see Bowen, Hodgdon, "He do Cressida in different voices," and LaBranche. I also draw on the performance theory and historiography that has begun to chart varying relations between theatre and gender from Athenian tragedy through the Elizabethan playhouse and *commedia dell'arte* to the Victorian music hall and contemporary performance art. I am indebted to several references not otherwise noted: Bassnett; Tracy Davis; Dolan; Jardine; Orgel, "Nobody's perfect"; and Zeitlin.

2   See Barber, Blair, and Rutter.

3   Such "negative feminism," however, characterizes the theatrical agenda of *l'écriture féminine* that Hélène Cixous sets forth in "Aller à la mer." See also the discussion in Féral and the critique of Féral in Freedman, 140–2. For an economical discussion of *l'écriture féminine*, see Jones.

4   The story of the onstage execution is traditionally told about the reign of Diocletian; on the legal status of Elizabethan boy actors, see Hillebrand; on the coercion of the pornographic film star, see the autobiography of Linda Lovelace and the discussion of it in Linda Williams, 112–13 and *passim*.

5   See Diamond, "*Gestus* and signature," and Maus. Recent full-length studies of the Restoration actress include Howe; of the eighteenth-century actress, Straub.

6   See Dash, especially 3–4 and 254. For a survey of choices that variants in the early texts offer several women's roles, see Urkowitz.

7   Playing Shakespeare is not, however, at least in the United States in the 1990s, a consistent or remunerative job of work. On the disappearance of classic theatre from the work of the working actor, see Berman.

8   The idea of "the presentation of self in everyday life," formulated by sociologist Erving Goffman, and developed by Elizabeth Burns, reemerges in numerous discussions of cultural theatricality in the English Renaissance. See for example Greenblatt, 1–3; Montrose, 53–7; and especially Agnew, 57–148. On the consequences of this blurred distinction, see George.

9   The *locus classicus* in critical studies of the *theatrum mundi* metaphor is Curtius; in the psychoanalytic study of masquerade, Rivière.

10   I am indebted to Kelly Ferguson for bringing this interview to my attention and to providing me with a copy of it.

11   For a survey of this criticism, see Jamieson.

12   I discussed Weimann's distinction between the *locus* and *platea* in "The High Roman fashion," where I was concerned with the historical relations of elite and popular traditions in the Elizabethan playhouse. I return to it here because it seems to me the single most useful concept that Elizabethan stage history has to offer contemporary Shakespearean theatre. For a recent full-length study of the Shakespearean clown, see Wiles.

13   On Brecht and clown theatre, see Gaskill, 47–51 and *passim*; and Schechter.

14   Shakespeare ran the risks of the unaccompanied boy actor so seldom that finding scenes and speeches for women remains a continual and chafing problem for acting workshops at every level. Since the exceptions tend to loom deceptively large, I offer the relevant statistics. The appendix to one widely used text, Robert Benedetti's *The Actor at Work*, offers a fairly complete list of Shakespearean duets. There are sixty-six for one woman and one

man; seventy-four for two men; and sixteen for two women (271–4). A popular anthology of Shakespearean monologues, Michael Earley and Philippa Keil's companion volumes of men's and women's soliloquies, also fairly complete, prints 101 monologues for men, fifty-six of which demand or permit the actor's presence alone on stage; in the volume of women's monologues, there are seventy-three speeches, including quite a few that have been cobbled together from duets and ten that are offered as "breeches parts," such as the choruses for *Henry V*. Only fifteen are not directed to an onstage auditor.

15 I am here indebted to remarks that Ctibor Turba and Judy Finelli made at the International Clown-Theatre Congress in Philadelphia, June 23–28, 1991, and to a paper that David Kastan presented to the Shakespeare Association of America.

16 Transformation is the player's art, but women's bodies have traditionally been seen as less "transformable" than men's. See Greenhalgh, 172.

17 One exception to Apte's rule can be found in the tales of the native population of Vancouver Island, recorded in Cameron, 107–14. Errors and omissions continue to mar the records of contemporary mime, circus, and *vaudeville nouveau*. Ron Jenkins's *Acrobats of the Soul*, for example, does not include a single woman. In a *New York Times* article on Bill Irwin and David Shiner's *Fool Moon*, Ann Hornaday reveals, with insouciant circularity, the rationale that underlies such errors and omissions: "It's also no accident that most clowns have been male . . . great clowns often bring a virile edge to their performance" (21). On women in other twentieth-century comic forms such as music hall and stand-up, see Banks and Swift; on women and comic play texts, Carlson.

18 The female clown has made one foray into such a venue, with the clownish Ganymede of Juliet Stevenson's Rosalind in Adrian Noble's 1985 *As You Like It*. See Stevenson and Shaw's discussion of Rosalind and Celia, 55–71. For a review of this production, see Roger Warren.

19 For a discussion of the presence of *commedia* characters in *Othello*, which includes a survey of earlier research on Shakespeare and *commedia*, see Faherty. On women and *commedia*, see McGill.

20 The quoted phrase is from a chapter title of Michael Bristol. Cf. Brecht: "There is only one way to fight authority . . . outlast it" ("*Geschichten von Herr Keuner*," *Prosa* 2, 106; quoted in Schechter, 56).

21 H. R. Courson made this observation in a paper read at "Shakespeare: Stage, Film, and Hypermedia," MIT, March 4–6, 1991.

22 Perhaps the only scholars patient enough to accompany the player in her work on Shakespeare's language are those textual critics who have interested themselves in the performance choices suggested by variant readings in the

early texts. See Michael Warren. For descriptions of exercises for "embodying the text," see Cicely Berry and Linklater.

23 Bal writes,

> To name this nameless character is to violate the biblical text. Not to name her is to violate her with the text . . . I feel it is not only acceptable, but necessary, to take some critical distance from the alienating anonymity of the character without, however, losing sight of the structure of subjectivity that it signifies. Therefore, I will give this woman a name, but a name which stresses her dependence and her state. (43)

24 Jackson, 64. See also Rackin, 220 n. 35. For a survey of the criticism on Joan as strumpet, see Jackson.

25 Cf. Clemen: "These strutting figures are, after all, not real persons but embodiments of limited functions for which they are the mouthpiece" ("Some aspects of style," 20–1).

26 Of the 2,251 lines of *Troilus and Cressida*, Chambers (whose tallies exclude prologues, epilogues, and interludes) counts only 186 or 8 percent in rhyme. See the tabulation in Wells and Taylor, 96.

27 Nor is rhyme otherwise common in soliloquies. After surveying a range of soliloquies, Warren D. Smith concludes that Shakespeare meticulously avoided rhyme in order to save it for exit cues (101–7). Smith's survey is largely based on men's monologues, and largely restricted to those of the variety Williams calls reflexive. In such speeches, rhyme does tend to be restricted to closing couplets such as Hamlet's "The play's the thing / Wherein I'll catch the conscience of the king." It is used more extensively in presentational prologues and choral intercalations such as Gower's tetrameter couplets or epilogues such as Pandarus's. It also appears more frequently in women's than men's soliloquies. Cressida and the Helenas of both *A Midsummer Night's Dream* and *All's Well That Ends Well* all have rhymed soliloquies, each with very different effects. For other responses to Cressida's rhymes, see Foakes, 144 and Hodgdon, "He do Cressida," 264–5. The most recent full-length investigation of the Shakespearean soliloquy is Wolfgang Clemen's *Shakespeare's Soliloquies*.

28 For a historical investigation of the play's sexual politics, see Wickham. For criticism from various other perspectives, see Abrams and the essays in Frey.

29 These feminine endings have been remarked chiefly as a metrical test to demonstrate Fletcher's authorship. (See Bertram, 218–33.) Their presence thus acquits Shakespeare of the charge of creating a character whose frank sexuality is so lawlessly levelling. The authorial source of Filia's poetic and rhetorical strategies is less significant here than their theatrical repercussions.

For a suggestive analogy, see McClary's discussion of the *avant garde* feminine ending in the musical cadences of a somewhat later period, 80–111.

30 Following Foucault, this early modern medicalization has received much attention from both historians and literary critics. For a discussion of madness and gender in Shakespeare that also surveys recent historical investigations, see Neely.

31 Thus Wright, for example, interprets Cressida's short line, "But now you have it, take it" (V. ii. 90), spoken after Diomedes takes Troilus's token from her during the eavesdropping scene, as a metrical slur on her character: Cressida "betrays her lover so gratuitously that the line misses a beat" (182). For me, the short line, here as elsewhere in Shakespeare, signals a distress that leaves the speaker unable to complete her thought formally.

32 Styan himself denies or at any rate mimimizes Brecht's influence (233–4). For other perspectives, see Gooch and Gaskill.

33 See also Dollimore, 63–9 and *passim*; Heinemann; McCullough; Sinfield, "History and power."

34 Whether or not Brecht is necessary for feminist theatre, he is not sufficient. Hence articles and chapters by feminist theorists of performance regularly bear titles like "Beyond Brecht," "Rethinking Brecht" (both Reinelt), and "Starting with Brecht" (Bennett). In "Brechtian theory/feminist theory," Elin Diamond calls for a gestic feminism through which Brechtian strategies would foreground gender as well as class (84–5). See also Pollack, 155–99.

35 Another example: Edward S. Brubaker, who directed *King John* at Ashland, assumes that "When Elinor, Constance, Blanch, the Bastard, and Austria fall into wrangling banter before the gates of Angiers, their manner should justify King Philip's rebuke, 'Women and fools, break off your conference' (2. 1. 150)" (168). In Deborah Warner's acclaimed production, however, Philip's rebuke was indeed unjustified, demonstrating that the hysteria was his own and, fortuitously, that the directorial assumption that Philip must be taken at his word arises from an ideological rather than an artistic imperative.

36 For descriptions of this production, see Ralph Berry, 61 and Bowen, 203.

37 For a different assessment of this production, see McLuskie, *Renaissance Dramatists*, 11–16.

38 Hugh Richmond's stage history of the play suggests that Filia's centrality is inscribed into the play text. It is indeed a wonderful role, and Stubbs's triumph in it followed a precedent set by Jean Forbes-Robinson at the Old Vic in 1928 and maintained by Jean Viner in the 1973 production of the York Theatre Royal, Suzanna Peter in the 1979 production at the Los Angeles Shakespeare Society of America, and Nancy Carlin in the 1985 Berkeley Shakespeare Festival (168–77).

39 Although Berger modifies his position somewhat in *Imaginary Audition*, I refer to the earlier essay, since he does not revise his remarks on *Macbeth*, which remain relevant to my purposes here. For a critique of the hierarchizing impulse in the phrase "text vs performance," see Hodgdon, "Parallel practices."

40 Since I first formulated these thoughts on *Macbeth*, performances and workshops of numerous mimes and clowns, especially Arina Isaacson, Bill Irwin, Geoff Hoyle, Jacques Lecoq, and Klauniada, have strengthened my sense of the vitality that contemporary clown theatre may bring to a modern Shakespearean *platea*. For discussions of this theatre, see Fo, R. G. Davis, Jenkins, Leabhart, Lecoq, and Schechter. See also Cousin on Footsbarn's *Hamlet* and *King Lear* and Cohn on Mnouchkine's *Le Théâtre Soleil*.

41 For a critique of Forman (and those who have relied on him), see Scragg.

42 On the politics of the court masque, see Orgel, *The Illusion of Power*.

43 On the historical shift in biological paradigms, see Keller and Laqueur.

44 For an argument that the soliloquy is intrinsically conservative, see Moretti.

45 Such was Nunn's conception for the production as Ian McKellan described it at "Images of Death: A Symposium on *Macbeth*, sponsered by the UCLA Center for Medieval and Renaissance Studies on May 15, 1987.

46 Marowitz's collage is one of several *avant garde* adaptations that debunks Macbeth's heroism by heightening Lady Macbeth's dominance and then shuddering visibly at its effects. See Cohn, *Modern Shakespearean Offshoots*, 60–105, especially 100–2.

47 For reviews of Mussmann's *M.A.C.B.E.T.H.*, see French, Fuchs, and Liebler.

48 For a discussion of Littlewood's Shakespeare productions, see Callaghan.

49 In an earlier version of this essay, I considered cross-casting Macbeth and Lady Macbeth, thinking that a female Macbeth and a male Lady Macbeth might challenge the masculinism of the Shakespearean *locus* as the Weyward Sisters challenge that of the *platea*. Since that time, there have been numerous experiments with cross-casting, most of which have been so unedifying that I now prefer to let the current conventions of the *locus* stand, while the Weyward Sisters play out their version from the *platea*. For reviews of cross-cast productions of Jacobean plays, see Diamond, "Lear"; Duncan-Jones; and Savitsky.

Works Cited

Abrams, Richard, "Gender confusion and sexual politics in *The Two Noble Kinsmen*," in James Redmond (ed.), *Drama, Sex, and Politics* (Cambridge, Cambridge University Press, 1985), 69–76.

Adelman, Janet, " 'Born of woman': fantasies of maternal power in *Macbeth*," in Marjorie Garber (ed.), *Cannibals, Witches, and Divorce: Estranging the Renaissance* (Baltimore, Johns Hopkins University Press, 1986), 90–121.

———, " 'This is and is not Cressid': the characterization of Cressida," in Shirley Nelson Garner, Claire Kahane, and Madelon Sprengnether (eds), *The (M)other Tongue: Essays in Feminist Psychoanalytic Interpretation* (Ithaca, Cornell University Press, 1985), 119–41.

Agnew, Jean-Christophe, *Worlds Apart: The Market and the Theater in Anglo-American Thought, 1550–1750* (Cambridge, Cambridge University Press, 1986).

Apte, Mahadev L., *Humor and Laughter: An Anthropological Approach* (Ithaca, Cornell University Press, 1985).

Bal, Mieke, *Death and Dissymetry: The Politics of Coherence in the Book of Judges* (Chicago, University of Chicago Press, 1988).

Banks, Morwenna and Swift, Amanda, *The Joke's on Us: Women in Comedy from Music Hall to the Present Day* (London, Pandora, 1987).

Barber, Frances, "Ophelia in *Hamlet*," in Russell Jackson and Robert Smallwood (eds), *Players of Shakespeare* 2, (Cambridge, Cambridge University Press, 1988), 137–49.

Bartholomeusz, Denis, *"Macbeth" and the Players* (Cambridge, Cambridge University Press, 1969).

Barton, John, *Playing Shakespeare* (London: Methuen, 1984).

Bassnett, Susan, "Struggling with the past: women's theatre in search of a history," *New Theatre Quarterly*, 5 (May 1989), 107–12.

Belsey, Catherine, *The Subject of Tragedy: Identity and Difference in Renaissance Drama* (London, Methuen, 1985).

Benedetti, Robert L., *The Actor at Work*, 4th edn (Englewood Cliffs, Prentice-Hall, 1986).

Bennett, Susan, *Theatre Audiences: A Theory of Production and Reception* (London, Routledge, 1990).

Berger, Harry, Jr, *Imaginary Audition: Shakespeare on Stage and Page* (Berkeley, University of California Press, 1989).

———, "Text against performance in Shakespeare: the example of *Macbeth*," *Genre*, 15 (1982), 49–79.

Berman, David, "Inventories," *American Theatre* (October, 1990), 7.

Berry, Cicely, *The Actor and his Text* (London, Harrup, 1987).

Berry, Ralph, *Changing Styles in Shakespeare* (London, Allen & Unwin, 1981).

Bertram, Paul, *Shakespeare and "The Two Noble Kinsmen"* (New Brunswick, NJ, Rutgers University Press, 1965).

Bingham, Dennis, "Jane Howell's first tetralogy: Brechtian break-out or just good television?" in J. C. Bulman and H. R. Coursen (eds), *Shakespeare on Television:*

An Anthology of Essays and Reviews (Hanover, NH, University Press of New England, 1988), 221–9.

Blau, Herbert, *The Audience* (Baltimore, Johns Hopkins University Press, 1990).

Blair, Rhoda, "Shakespeare and the feminist actor," *Women and Performance*, 2 (1985), 18–26.

Bowen, Barbara E., *"Troilus and Cressida* on the stage," in William Shakespeare, *The History of Troilus and Cressida*, Daniel Seltzer ed. (The Signet Classic Shakespeare, New York, Signet, 1988).

Brecht, Bertolt, *The Messingkauf Dialogues*, trans. John Willet (London, Methuen, 1965).

Bristol, Michael, *Carnival and Theatre: Plebeian Culture and the Structure of Authority in Renaissance England* (New York, Routledge, 1985).

Brook, Peter, *The Empty Space* (New York, Atheneum, 1968).

Bruaker, Edward S., "Staging *King John*: a director's observations," in Deborah T. Curren-Aquino (ed.), *"King John": New Perspectives* (Newark, University of Delaware Press, 1989), 164–72.

Burns, Elizabeth, *Theatricality: A Study of Convention in the Theatre and in Social Life* (London, Longman, 1972).

Callaghan, Dympna, "Shakespeare at the fun palace: Joan Littlewood," in Marianne Novy (ed.), *Cross-Cultural Performances: Differences in Women's Re-Visions of Shakespeare* (Urbana, University of Illinois Press, 1993), 108–26.

Cameron, Anne, *Daughters of Copper Woman* (Vancouver, Press Gang Publishers, 1981).

Carlson, Susan, *Women and Comedy: Rewriting the British Theatrical Tradition* (Ann Arbor, University of Michigan Press, 1991).

Case, Sue-Ellen, *Feminism and Theatre* (New York, Methuen, 1988).

Chambers, Edward, *The Elizabethan Stage*, 4 vols (Oxford, Oxford University Press, 1923).

Cixous, Hélène, "Aller à la mer," trans. Barbara Kerslake, *Modern Drama*, 27 (1984), 546–8.

Clemen, Wolfgang, *Shakespeare's Soliloquies*, trans. Charity Scott Stokes (London, Methuen, 1987).

——, "Some aspects of style in the *Henry VI* plays," in Philip Edwards, Inga-Stina Ewbank, and G. K. Hunter (eds), *Shakespeare's Styles: Essays in Honour of Kenneth Muir* (Cambridge, Cambridge University Press, 1980).

Clément, Catherine, *Opéra; or, the Undoing of Women*, trans. Betsy Wing (Minneapolis, University of Minnesota Press, 1988).

Cohn, Ruby, "Ariane Mnouchkine: playwright of a collective," in Enoch Brater (ed.), *Feminine Focus: The New Women Playwrights* (Oxford, Oxford University Press, 1989), 53–63.

Cohn, Ruby, *Modern Shakespearean Offshoots* (Princeton, Princeton University Press, 1976).

Coursen, H. R., "The gravedigger's scene on film and TV," paper delivered at "Shakespeare: Film, Stage, Hypermedia," MIT, March 5–6, 1992.

Cousin, Geraldine, "Shakespeare from scratch: the Footsbarn *Hamlet* and *King Lear*," *New Theatre Quarterly*, 1 (1985), 105–27.

Curtius, Ernst Robert, *European Literature and the Latin Middle Ages*, trans. Willard R. Trask (Princeton, Princeton University Press, 1973).

Dash, Irene G., *Wooing, Wedding and Power: Women in Shakespeare's Plays* (New York, Columbia University Press, 1981).

Davis, Tracy C., "Questions for a feminist methodology in theatre history," in Thomas Postlewait and Bruce A. McConachie (eds), *Interpreting the Theatrical Past: Essays in the Historiography of Performance* (Iowa City, University of Iowa Press, 1989), 59–81.

Davis, R. G., *The San Francisco Mime Troupe: The First Ten Years* (Palo Alto, Ramparts Press, 1975).

Diamond, Elin, "Brechtian Theory/feminist theory: toward a gestic feminist criticism." *The Drama Review*, 32 (1988), 82–94.

——, "*Gestus* and signature in Aphra Behn's *The Rover*," *English Literary History*, 56 (1989), 519–41.

——, Review of *Lear* (Mabou Mines), *Theatre Journal* (December, 1990), 481–4.

Dolan, Jill, *The Feminist Spectator as Critic* (Ann Arbor, UMI Research Press, 1988).

Dollimore, Jonathan, *Radical Tragedy: Religion, Ideology and Power in the Drama of Shakespeare and his Contemporaries* (Chicago, University of Chicago Press, 1984).

Duncan-Jones, Katherine, Review of *The Malcontent* (John Marston), Latchmere Theatre, Battersea, London, *Times Literary Supplement* (May 12–18, 1989), 514.

Eagleton, Terry, *William Shakespeare* (Oxford, Basil Blackwell, 1986).

Earley, Michael and Keil, Philippa (eds), *Soliloquy! The Shakespeare Monologues (Men)* (New York, Applause Theatre Books, 1988).

——, *Soliloquy! The Shakespeare Monologues (Women)* (New York, Applause Theatre Books, 1988).

Evans, Gareth Lloyd, "*Macbeth*: 1946–80 at Stratford-upon-Avon," in John Russell Brown (ed.), *Focus on "Macbeth"* (London, Routledge, 1982), 87–109.

Evans, G. Blakemore (ed.), *The Riverside Shakespeare* (Boston, Houghton Mifflin, 1974).

Faherty, Teresa J., "*Othello dell'Arte*: the presence of *commedia* in Shakespeare's tragedy," *Theatre Journal*, 43 (May 1991), 179–94.

Féral, Josette, "Performance and theatricality: the subject demystified," trans. Terese Lyons, *Modern Drama*, 25 (1982), 170–81.

Fo, Dario, *The Tricks of the Trade*, trans. Joe Farrell (New York, Routledge, 1991).

Foakes, R. A., "*Troilus and Cressida* reconsidered," *University of Toronto Quarterly*, 32 (1963), 142–54.

Freedman, Barbara, *Staging the Gaze: Postmodernism, Psychoanalysis, and Shakespearean Comedy* (Ithaca, Cornell University Press, 1991).

Freeman, Neil (ed.), *The Tragedie of Macbeth* (Toronto, Folio Scripts, 1990).

French, Marilyn, Review of *M.A.C.B.E.T.H* (Time and Space Limited). *Ms* (March/April 1991), 68–70.

Frey, Charles (ed.), *Shakespeare, Fletcher, and "The Two Noble Kinsmen"* (Columbia, University of Missouri Press, 1989).

Fuchs, Elinor, Review of *M.A.C.B.E.T.H* (Time and Space Limited), *The Village Voice* (November 27, 1990).

Gaskill, William, *A Sense of Direction: Life at the Royal Court Theatre* (New York, Limelight Editions, 1990).

George, David E. R., "Letter to a poor actor," *New Theatre Quarterly*, 2 (1986), 352–63.

Goffman, Erving, *The Presentation of Self in Everyday Life* (New York, Pelican, 1971).

Goldman, Michael, *Acting and Action in Shakespearean Tragedy* (Princeton, Princeton University Press, 1985).

——, *The Actor's Freedom* (New York, Viking Press, 1975).

Gooch, Steve, *All Together Now: An Alternative View of Theatre and the Community* (London, Methuen, 1984).

Gordon, Mel, *Lazzi: The Comic Routines of the Commedia dell'Arte* (New York, Performing Arts Journal Publications, 1983).

Greenblatt, Stephen, *Renaissance Self-Fashioning* (Chicago, University of Chicago Press, 1980).

Greene, Gayle, "Shakespeare's Cressida: 'a kind of self'," in Carolyn Ruth Swift Lenz, Gayle Greene, and Carol Thomas Neely (eds), *The Woman's Part* (Urbana, University of Illinois Press, 1980), 133–49.

Greenhalgh, Susan, "Occupying the empty space," in Ann Thompson and Helen Wilcox (eds), *Teaching Women: Feminism and English studies* (Manchester, Manchester University Press, 1989), 170–9.

Hattaway, Michael (ed.), *The First Part of King Henry VI. The New Cambridge Shakespeare* (Cambridge, Cambridge University Press, 1990).

Heinemann, Margot, 'How Brecht read Shakespeare," in Jonathan Dollimore and Alan Sinfield (eds), *Political Shakespeare* (Ithaca, Cornell University Press, 1985), 202–30.

Helms, Lorraine, " 'The High Roman fashion': sacrifice and suicide on the Shakespearean stage," *PMLA* (May, 1992), 554–65.

Hillebrand, Harold, *The Child Actors* (1926) (New York, Russell & Russell, 1964).

Hodgdon, Barbara, "He do Cressida in different voices," *English Literary Renaissance*, 20 (1990), 254–86.

——, "Parallel practices, or the un-necessary difference," *The Kenyon Review*, n.s. 7 (1985), 57–65.

Holderness, Graham, "Radical potentiality and institutional closure: Shakespeare in film and television," in Jonathan Dollimore and Alan Sinfield (eds), *Political Shakespeare* (Ithaca, Cornell University Press, 1985), 182–201.

Hornaday, Anne, "Once again the clowning gets physical," *New York Times* (April 11, 1993), 21.

Howe, Elizabeth. *The First English Actresses* (Cambridge, Cambridge University Press, 1992).

Jackson, Gabriele Bernhard, "Topical ideology: witches, Amazons, and Shakespeare's Joan of Arc," *English Literary Renaissance*, 18 (1988), 40–65.

Jamieson, Michael, "Shakespeare's celibate stage," in Gerald Eades Bentley (ed.), *The Seventeenth-Century Stage* (Chicago, University of Chicago Press, 1968), 70–93.

Jardine, Lisa, *Still Harping on Daughters: Women and Drama in the Age of Shakespeare*, 2nd edn (New York, Columbia University Press, 1989).

Jenkins, Ron, *Acrobats of the Soul: Comedy and Virtuosity in Contemporary American Theatre* (New York, Theatre Communications Group, 1988).

Jones, Ann Rosalind, "Writing the body: toward an understanding of *l'écriture féminine*," in Judith Newton and Deborah Rosenfelt (eds), *Feminist Criticism and Social Change: Sex, Class and Race in Literature and Culture* (New York, Methuen, 1985), 86–101.

Kastan, David Scott, " 'Clownes shoulde speake disorderlye': mongrel tragicomedy and the unitary state," paper presented to the Shakespeare Association of America, 1989.

Keller, Evelyn Fox, *Reflections on Gender and Science* (New Haven, Yale University Press, 1985).

Kott, Jan, *The Memory of the Body: Essays on Theatre and Death* (Evanston, Northwestern University Press, 1992).

Kristeva, Julia, "Woman can never be defined," in Elaine Marks and Isabelle de Courtivron (eds), *New French Feminisms: An Anthology* (New York, Schocken, 1981).

LaBranche, Linda Berning, "The theatrical dimension of *Troilus and Cressida*," Northwestern University dissentation, 1984.

Laqueur, Thomas, *Making Sex: Body and Gender from the Greeks to Freud* (Berkeley, University of California Press, 1990).

Leabhart, Thomas, *Modern and Post-Modern Mime. Modern Dramatists* (New York, St Martin's Press, 1989).

Lecoq, Jacques, *Le Théâtre du geste: mimes et acteurs sous la direction de Jacques Lecoq* (Paris, Bordas, 1987).

Liebler, Naomi Conn, Review of *M.A.C.B.E.T.H* (Time and Space Limited), *Shakespeare Bulletin*, 9 (1991), 89.

Linklater, Kristin, *Freeing Shakespeare's Voice* (New York, Theatre Communications Group, 1992).

Lomax, Marion, *Stage Images and Traditions: Shakespeare to Ford* (Cambridge, Cambridge University Press, 1987).

Lovelace, Linda and Mike McGrady, *Ordeal* (New York, Berkley Books, 1981).

Marowitz, Charles, *The Marowitz Shakespeare* (New York, Drama Book Specialists, 1978).

Maus, Katherine Eisaman, " 'Playhouse flesh and blood': sexual ideology and the restoration actress," *English Literary History*, 46 (1979), 595–617.

McClary, Susan, *Feminine Endings: Music, Gender, and Sexuality* (Minneapolis, University of Minnesota Press, 1991).

McCullough, Christopher J., "The Cambridge connection: towards a materialist theatre practice," in Graham Holderness (ed.), *The Shakespeare Myth* (Manchester, University of Manchester Press, 1988), 112–21.

McGill, Kathleen, "Women and performance: the development of improvisation by the sixteenth century *commedia dell'arte*," *Theatre Journal*, 43 (1991), 58–69.

McGrath, John, *A Good Night Out/Popular Theatre: Audience, Class, and Form* (London, Eyre Methuen, 1983).

McLuskie, Kathleen, *Renaissance Dramatists* (Atlantic Highlands, NJ, Humanities Press, 1989).

——, "The patriarchal bard: feminist consciousness and Shakespeare–*King Lear* and *Measure for Measure*," in Jonathan Dollimore and Alan Sinfield (eds), *Political Shakespeare* (Ithaca, Cornell University Press, 1985), 88–108.

Montrose, Louis, "The purpose of playing: reflections on a Shakespearean anthropology," *Helios*, n.s. 7 (1979–80), 51–74.

Moretti, Franco, " 'A huge eclipse': tragic form and the deconsecration of sovereignty," *Genre*, 15 (1982), 7–40.

Mulvey, Laura, "Visual pleasure and narrative cinema," *Screen*, 16 (1975); reprinted in Constance Penley (ed.), *Feminism and Film Theory* (New York, Routledge, 1988), 57–79.

Neely, Carol Thomas, " 'Documents in madness': reading madness and gender in Shakespeare's tragedies and early modern culture," *Shakespeare Quarterly*, 42 (1991), 315–38.

Orgel, Stephen, "Nobody's perfect; or, why did the English stage take boys for women?" *South Atlantic Quarterly*, 88 (1989), 7–29.

——, *The Illusion of Power: Political Theatre in the English Renaissance* (Berkeley, University of California Press, 1975).

Papp, Joseph, "Directing *Troilus and Cressida*," in Bernard Beckerman and Joseph Papp (eds), *Troilus and Cressida: The Festival Shakespeare* (New York, Macmillan, 1967).

Parker, Patricia, *Literary Fat Ladies: Rhetoric, Gender, Property* (London, Methuen, 1987).

Pollack, Griselda, *Vision and Difference: Femininity, Feminism, and the Histories of Art* (London, Routledge, 1988).

Rackin, Phyllis, *Stages of History: Shakespeare's English Chronicles* (Ithaca, Cornell University Press, 1990).

Reinelt, Janelle, "Rethinking Brecht: deconstruction, feminism and the politics of form," *Brecht Yearbook*, 15 (1990), 99–107.

——, "Beyond Brecht: Britain's new feminist drama," *Theatre Journal*, 38 (1986), 154–63.

Richmond, Hugh, "Performance as criticism: *The Two Noble Kinsmen*," in Charles Frey (ed.), *Shakespeare, Fletcher, and "The Two Noble Kinsmen"* (Columbia, University of Missouri Press, 1989), 163–85.

Rivière, Joan, "Womenliness as masquerade," reprinted in Victor Burgin, James Donald, and Cora Kaplan (eds), *Formations of Fantasy* (London, Methuen, 1986), 35–44.

Roach, Joseph A., "Power's body: the inscription of morality as style," in Thomas Postlewait and Bruce A. McConachie (eds), *Interpreting the Theatrical Past: Essays in the Historiography of Performance* (Iowa City, University of Iowa Press, 1989), 99–118.

Rosenberg, Marvin, *The Masks of Macbeth* (Berkeley, University of California Press, 1978).

Rutter, Carol, with Sinead Cusack, Paola Dionisotti, Fiona Shaw, Juliet Stevenson, and Hariet Walter, *Clamorous Voices: Shakespeare's Women Today*, ed. Faith Evans (London, The Women's Press, 1988).

Salgado, Gamini, *Eyewitnesses to Shakespeare: First Hand Accounts of Performances 1590–1890* (New York, Harper & Row, 1975).

Savitsky, Susan, Review of *The Taming of the Shrew* (Quinapalus Theatre Company), *Shakespeare Bulletin* (July/August, 1989), 16–17.

Schecter, Joel, *Durov's Pig: Clowns, Politics, and Theatre* (New York, Theatre Communications Group, 1985).

Scragg, Leah, "Macbeth on horseback," *Shakespeare Survey*, 26 (1973), 81–88.

Spencer, Hazleton, "D'Avenant's *Macbeth* and Shakespeare's," *PMLA*, 40 (1925), 619–44.

Showalter, Elaine, "Representing Ophelia: women, madness, and the responsibilities of feminist criticism," in Patricia Parker and Geoffrey Hartman (eds), *Shakespeare and the Question of Theory* (New York, Methuen, 1985), 77–94.

Sinfield, Alan, "Royal Shakespeare: theatre and the making of ideology," in Jonathan Dollimore and Alan Sinfield (eds), *Political Shakespeare* (Ithaca, Cornell University Press, 1985), 130–81.

——, "History and power," program notes for *The Plantagenets*, Royal Shakespeare Company, dir. Adrian Noble, the Barbican, London, 1989.

Smith, Warren D., *Shakespeare's Playhouse Practice: A Handbook* (Hanover, NH, University Press of New England, 1975).

Stevenson, Juliet and Shaw, Fiona, "Rosalind and Celia," in Russell Jackson and Robert Smallwood (eds), *Players of Shakespeare 2* (Cambridge, Cambridge University Press, 1988).

Stoppard, Tom, *Rosencrantz and Guildenstern Are Dead* (New York, Grove Press, 1967).

Straub, Kristina, *Sexual Suspects: Eighteenth-Century Players and Sexual Ideology* (Princeton, Princeton University Press, 1992).

Stubbs, Imogen, "An actor's diary: a view from the stage," *Drama* 162 (1986), 33–54.

Styan, J. L., *The Shakespeare Revolution* (Cambridge, Cambridge University Press, 1977).

Towson, John H., *Clowns* (New York, Hawthorn Books, 1976).

"Troilus and Cressida," program notes for *Troilus and Cressida*, the Stratford Festival, dir. David William, Avon Theatre, Stratford, Ontario, 1987.

Trussler, Simon, "Commentary," program notes for *The Two Noble Kinsmen*, Royal Shakespeare Company, dir. Barry Kyle, Swan Theatre, Stratford-upon-Avon, 1986.

Urkowitz, Steven, "Five women eleven ways: changing images of Shakespearean characters in the earliest texts," In Warner Habicht, D. J. Palmer, and Roger Pringle (eds), *Images of Shakespeare: Proceedings of the Third Congress of the International Shakespeare Association, 1986* (Newark, University of Delaware Press, 1988), 292–304.

Warren, Michael, "The theatricalization of text: Beckett, Jonson, Shakespeare," *The Library Chronicle* (Austin, The University of Texas, 1990), 38–59.

Warren, Roger, "Shakespeare in Britain, 1985," *Shakespeare Quarterly*, 37 (1986), 114–20.

Weimann, Robert, *Shakespeare and the Popular Tradition in the Theatre*, ed. Robert Schwartz (Baltimore, Johns Hopkins University Press, 1978).

Wells, Stanley and Taylor, Gary, *William Shakespeare: A Textual Companion* (Oxford, Clarendon Press, 1987).

Wickham, Glynne, "*The Two Noble Kinsmen* or *A Midsummer Night's Dream*, Part II?" in George Hibbard (ed.), *Elizabethan Theatre VII* (Hamden, Archon Books, 1980), 167–96.

Wiles, David, *Shakespeare's Clown: Actor and Text in the Elizabethan Playhouse* (Cambridge, Cambridge University Press, 1987).

Williams, Linda, *Hard Core* (Berkeley, University of California Press, 1989).

Williams, Raymond, *Writing in Society* (London, Verso, n.d.).

——, *Modern Tragedy* (Stanford, Stanford University Press, 1966).

Woddis, Carole, "A woman's role," *Plays and Players* (October, 1987), 14–15.

Worthen, William, "The rhetoric of performance criticism," *Shakespeare Quarterly*, 40 (1989), 441–55.

Wright, George T., *Shakespeare's Metrical Art* (Berkeley, University of California Press, 1988).

Yoder, R. A., " 'Sons and daughters of the game': an essay on Shakespeare's *Troilus and Cressida*," *Shakespeare Survey*, 25 (1972), 11–25.

Zeitlin, Froma I., "Playing the Other: theatre, theatricality, and the feminine in Greek drama," in John J. Winkler and Froma I. Zeitlin (eds), *Nothing to Do with Dionysus? Athenian Drama in its Social Context* (Princeton, Princeton University Press, 1990), 63–96.

Index

absolutism: and capitalism 71; and
  desire 71, 72, 73–4, 84;
  monarchy vs patriarchy 87; and
  paternalism 43
actors: boys in female role 34,
  108–12, 143–4 (n14); female
  105–6, 116; freedom 104–5,
  112; liminality 135; *see also*
  clowns
Adelman, Janet 41, 131–2
adultery 17–18
agency 10, 20
agrarian revolution 25–6, 53
  (n26)
Anatomie of Abuses, The (Stubbes)
  13, 18, 32
Angelo, *Measure for Measure* 45
Annis, Francesca 127
antihistories 7
Archer, Ian 11, 30
authority, comic inversion 76, 77

Baker, Herschel 35
Bankside 29, 30
Barton, John 127
Becon, Thomas 17–18
Beier A. L. 25

Belsey, Catherine 2–3, 91,
  110–11, 123
Berger, Harry 131, 136
Bertram, Paul 122–3
Betterton, Thomas 135
Bianca, *Othello* 47–50
Bingham, Dennis 127
Blau, Herbert 105, 107
Bowen, Barbara 128
boy actors 34, 108–12, 143–4
  (n14)
Brabantio, *Othello* 47
Brecht, Bertolt 111, 126, 146
  (n34)
Bridewell 23–4, 30, 31
Bristol, Michael 35, 118
Brook, Peter 139, 140
Brooke, Arthur 59
brothels: conditions 13;
  Elizabethan and Jacobean 30; in
  London 29–30; profitability
  30; regulations 23–4; and social
  instability 52 (n13); *see also*
  prostitution
Burford, E. J. 29, 30, 31

capitalism: and absolutism 71; and

family 68, 95 (n23); and
feudalism 93 (n16); historical
96 (n25); and marriage 82
*Capitalism, the Family and Personal
Life* (Zaretsky) 62
Capulet, *Romeo and Juliet* 76–7,
82, 83
caricature 106, 109
carnivalesque 35–6, 38, 138–9
Cassio, *Othello* 47–8
Catholic Church: and prostitution
14–15
Clément, Catherine 105
clowns: and actor's freedom 112;
and death 114, 116; direct
address 110; female 116, 118,
125, 139; and femininity
112–14; hungers 112, 129;
platea 115; Pompey 43–4
Coffey, Peggy 128
Columbine, *Othello* 114
commedia dell'arte 113, 140
commodification, of female sexuality
and labour 12, 20, 21, 45, 105
commoners: and elite 35–6;
history plays 33–6; *Measure for
Measure* 42
Conversion of an English Courtizen, The
(Greene) 19–21
courtly love 15, 62
Cressida, *Troilus and Cressida* 102,
103, 104, 119–21, 128
Cressy, David 64–6
critical discourse, and theatrical
practice 102–3
cross-casting 109, 147 (n49)
cultural materialism 34
cultural studies, feminist 59–60
culture: and desire 59–60, 71–2,
88; elitist 5–6; feminist studies
10, 59–60, 63–4; gender 8,

135; history 7; and identity
10–11; and sexuality 47
Cusack, Sinead 137

D'Avenant, Sir William 132, 135
Davies, Howard 128
Dekker, Thomas 12
Dench, Judi 136
Desdemona, *Othello* 46–7, 113–14
desire: and absolutism 71, 72,
73–4, 84; ahistoricized 64–5,
67–8; and coercion 41; cultural
construction 59–60, 71–2, 88;
determinism and disruption 90
(n10); Donne
97 (n34); and family 62;
female 84–6; fragmented
89–90 (n10); idealized 80–1;
male 11–12, 14, 15, 18, 21,
119; materialist history 71–2;
mutuality 81; new historicist
readings 3–4; and postmodern
present 69–72; refigured
72–3; sexual 80–1; social
history 64–5; transhistorical
61, 62–4; *see also* sexuality
destitution 26–7, 28
directors, female roles 106
displacement: agrarian revolution
25–6, 53 (n26); economic 25;
in *Othello* 48
Dollimore, Jonathan 42, 48
Donne, John 97 (n34)
Downes, John 135

Eagleton, Terry 131
editorial history 49–50
Edward VI, king of England 23,
30
elite: and commoners 35–6
Elizabeth, queen of England 30

embodying of text   104–8
Emilia, *Othello*   46, 49, 113–14
English Society 1580–1680
   (Wrightson)   66–7
Erasmus   16–17
eroticism: and gender   89–90
   (n10); maternal   84–5; *Troilus
   and Cressida*   120
Escalus, *Romeo and Juliet*   73–5,
   77–9, 87–8
essentialism   10
exogamy   76

Falstaff, Sir John   35–7
family: and capitalism   68, 95
   (n23); desire   62; exogamous
   76; feudal   75; in history
   65–6; naturalized   66–7;
   nuclear   79–84, 95 (n23);
   patriarchal   64; Protestantism
   65–6; psychoanalytic view   68;
   social history   65; as unit of
   production   95–6 (n25)
Family, Sex and Marriage, The (Stone)
   65–6
Fashioning Feminity (Newman)
   69–70
female impersonation   106, 108
female roles: as caricatures   106,
   109; directors   106; *locus*   111;
   see also boy actors
female sexuality: assigned   3;
   commodified   12, 20, 21, 45,
   105; cultural images   47;
   dangers of   17; demonized   11,
   19; and femininity   79; Filia
   145–6 (n29); and male desire
   18; masculine fear   51; and
   passivity   16; repressed   18; *see
   also* desire, female
female virtue   18–19

femininity: acting   105–6; and
   clowning   112–14; demonic
   132; and sexuality   79
feminist cultural studies   10,
   59–60, 63–4
feminist historiography   8, 9–10
feminist materialist approach   2–3,
   4, 8, 9
feudalism: and capitalism   93
   (n16); and state   72–9
Filia, *The Two Noble Kinsmen*
   122–5, 129–30; *locus*   124, 125;
   platea   123, 125; sexuality
   145–6 (n29); soliloquies   122–5
Fo, Dario   112
Forman, Simon   133–4
Foucault, Michel   7, 8
Freeman, Neil   134
Freud, Sigmund: patriarchy   63–4

gender   2, 7–8; and culture   8,
   135; and eroticism   89–90
   (n10); and hierarchy   8; and
   sexuality   63, 91–2 (n11)
Goldman, Michael   103, 104–5
Good Night Out, A (McGrath)   141
Gosson, Stephen   29
Gauda, Francis   33
Gouge, William   83–4
Granville-Barker, Harley   50
Greenblatt, Stephen   70–1, 94–5
   (n20), 95 (n22)
Greene, Robert   19–21
Griffiths, Paul   24, 30

Harrison, William   31–2
Hartmann, Heidi   2
Haselkorn, Anne   25, 32
Hattaway, Michael   119
Helen of Troy   19
Henry II, king of England   14

Henry IV, Parts 1 and 2 33–41
Henry VI, Part 1 115–19, 126–7
Henry VII, king of England 23
Henry VIII, king of England 22
historicism: *see* new historicism
historiography: feminist 8, 9–10;
 and postmodernism 69; and
 psychoanalysis 89, (n9)
history: as cultural analysis 7; and
 new historicism 71; postmodern
 approach 69–71; and
 psychoanalysis 62–9, 93–4
 (n17), 94–5 (n20); as teleology
 66
Holderness, Graham 126
Homely against whordom, An (Becon)
 17–18
homoeroticism 73–4
homosexuality 60
Honest Whore, The (Dekker) 12
Howard, Jean 37, 40, 95 (n22)
Howell, Jane 126–7

Iago, *Othello* 46, 47–8
identity 10–11, 60, 79
ideology: kingship 34–5;
 patriarchy 128–9; romantic
 love 60–2, 72, 88; sexuality
 42; tragic endings 86–8
improvisation 140
Inglis, Fred 4–5
interiority 110, 111, 121

Jailer's Daughter *see* Filia
Jardine, Alice 69
jealously, male 46
Joan of Arc 115–19; as clown
 116, 118; liminality 118;
 platea 118; soliloquy 116, 117
Juliet, *Measure for Measure* 45
Juliet, *Romeo and Juliet* 80–6

Julius Caesar 13

Kahn, Coppélia 75
Karras, Ruth Mazzo 24, 44
Kelso, Ruth 15
Kemble, Fanny 136
Kermode, Frank 86–7
King Lear 22, 114
kingship: ideology 34–5
Kristeva, Julia 61, 104
Kyle, Barry 129

Lapotaire, Jane 127
Laslett, Peter 82, 93 (n15)
Latimer, Bishop 30
lazzi 140
liminality: actors 135; Joan of
 Arc 118; *Macbeth* 138;
 witches 131
literary criticism: feminist 5;
 Marxist 91 (n11); political 5
Littlewood, Joan 141
locus 143 (n12); Cressida 120;
 Filia 124; and *platea* 110, 111
London, Renaissance: Bankside 29,
 30; Bridewell 23–4, 30, 31;
 brothels 29–30; Southwark
 23, 29, 31; underclass 39–40
love: courtly 15, 62; extra-marital
 60; Platonic 15; Puritan ideals
 64–5; romantic 59–62, 68, 69,
 72, 80, 88; sexual 3–4, 69;
 unconstrained 79–84; *see also*
 marriage
Love in the Western World
 (Rougement) 60

M.A.C.B.E.T.H. (Mussmann) 137
Macbeth, Lady 137
Macbeth: liminality 138; masque
 134–5; post-feminist 137;

Restoration production 135; sexual politics 131–2; soliloquy 136, 137; witches 130–1, 133–4; *see also* Weyward Sisters
Macbeth, A (Marowitz) 136–7
Macfarlane, Alan 67–8
McGrath, John 141
McKellen, Ian 136
MacLean, Ian 15
McLuskie, Kathleen 19–20, 41–2, 108
MacOwen, Michael 136
marginality 10, 11, 42
Mariana, *Measure for Measure* 45
market economy and displacement 25
Marowitz, Charles 136–7
marriage: and capitalism 82; companionate 67; economic conflicts 81–2, 83–4; enforced 79–80; exogamous 76; freedom of choice 81, 83; Puritan doctrine 32–3, 79–80; romantic 80
Marriage and Love in England 1300–1840 (Macfarlane) 67
Marxism 2, 71–2
Marxist criticism 91 (n11)
Masks of Macbeth, The (Rosenberg) 132
masque and *Macbeth* 134–5
masquerade 107
materialism: cultural 34; feminist 2–3, 4, 8, 9; historical 71–2
materialist criticism and psychoanalysis 90–2 (n11)
Measure for Measure 41–6
Mercutio, *Romeo and Juliet* 61, 73
Mitchell, Juliet 63, 91 (n11)
Moses and Monotheism (Freud) 63
Mulvey, Laura 108

Mussmann, Linda 137

naming 33–4, 79
Neely, Carol 10
new historicism 3–4, 34, 71, 95 (n22)
Newman, Karen 69–70
Noble, Adrian 137
nuclear family 79–84, 95 (n23)
Nunn, Trevor 136
Nurse, *Romeo and Juliet* 83, 82–6, 112

Oedipus complex 63
Ophelia, *Hamlet* 112, 114
Othello 13, 46–51; clowns 113; editorial history 49–50; feminist readings 47; masculinity 46–7; psychoanalytic approach 94–5 (n20)
Overdone, Mistress 42, 43–4, 45, 46

Papp, Joseph 127
Parker, Patricia 114–15
paternalism and absolutism 43
patriarchy: and feminism 63–4; ideology 128–9; and monarchy 87; post-Reformation 87; and psychoanalysis 63–4; Renaissance 8; on Shakespearean stage 106; and state 72–9
Pepys, Samuel 135
platea 143 (n12); clowning 115; Filia 123, 125; Joan of Arc 118; and *locus* 110, 111, 143 (n12); rough theatre 139; and soliloquy 110–11; Weyward Sisters 132
Playing Shakespeare (Barton) 127

Pompey, *Measure for Measure* 43–4,
45
Poor Law (1601) 31
Porter, Joseph 61
postmodernism 69–72
program notes, and
performances 128–9
prostitutes: carnivalesque 35–6,
38; class consciousness 37–8;
Henry IV, Parts 1 and 2 33–41;
marginalized 11, 42, 44;
Measure for Measure 41–6;
Othello 46–51; social history
11, 12; as stereotypes 34,
40–1, 46; terminology used 12;
textual traces 24–5
prostitution: Church's attitude
14–15; consumers 19; and
economic displacement 25,
28–9; economics of 46, 51; and
female desire 3; as female
entrepreneurship 40; harshness
17; institutionalized 29; moral
inquiries 13–14; *Othello* 94–5
(n20); punishment for 31–3;
reforming 17; Renaissance
representations 12–25; and
scapegoats 33; in Shakespeare's
Vienna 42; socio-economic
reasons 12, 13, 46, 51; supply
and demand 44; suppressed
23; as threat 17–18
Protestantism and family 65–6
Pryce, Jonathan 137
psychoanalysis: and family 68; and
historiography 89 (n9); and
history 62–9, 93–4 (n17),
94–5 (n20); and materialist
criticism 90–2 (n11); and
patriarchy 63–4; and
postmodernism 69–71;

Renaissance studies 64;
universalism 64
'Psychoanalysis and Renaissance
Culture' (Greenblatt) 70
puritanism: love and marriage
32–3, 64–5, 79–80

Quickly, Mistress 35–8

Rackin, Phyllis 34, 35–6
Rame, Franca 141
reflexive: and generic
soliloquies 120, 121
Renaissance England: female
sexuality 12; labour conditions
and social displacements 22–33;
London underclass 39–40;
psychoanalytic approach 64;
women depicted as wives/whores
12–22
Renaissance literary studies 64, 69
replication 62
Restoration: *Macbeth* 132, 135
Rewriting the Renaissance 9
Ridley, M. R. 49–50
romantic love: ideology 60–2, 72,
88; and marriage 80; and sexual
passion 69; transhistorical
59–60, 68; *see also* love
Romeo and Juliet: family, nuclear
79–84; female desire 84–6;
homoeroticism 61; ideology of
romantic love 62, 88; patriarchy
vs monarchy 72–9; sexual
desire 62, 63, 71–2; sources
59; tragic ending 86–8
Rosenberg, Marvin 132, 135
Rosencranz and Guilderstern Are Dead
(Stoppard) 138
Rougement, Denis de 60
Rutter, Carol 137

Salgado, Gamini   14–15, 31
School of Abuse, The (Gosson)   29
Scott, Joan   2, 7–8, 9–10
sexism   126–7
sexual knowledge   85–6
sexuality: distrust   41; feared   14;
   and gender   63, 91–2 (n11);
   ideological struggle   42; *see also*
   female sexuality
Shakespeare: female characters
   108; hierarchy of roles   108;
   productions   127–30, 131–7;
   prostitutes in   33–51; theatrical
   practices   126; *see also individual*
   plays
Shakespeare and the Popular Tradition
   (Weimann)   110
Shaw, Fiona   106
Showalter, Elaine   106, 107
Smith, Bruce   74
social history: desire   64–5;
   essentialist   71; family model
   65; prostitutes   11, 12
social order, revolutionized   25–6
soliloquy   103–4, 110; boy actors
   109–10, 143–4 (n14); Cressida
   119–21; Filia   122–5; Joan of
   Arc   116, 117; *Macbeth*   136,
   137; *platea*   110–11; rhyming
   119–21, 145 (n27)
Southwark   23, 29, 31
state centralization, and feudalism
   72–9
Stevenson, Juliet   128
Stockholder, Kay   75–6
Stone, Lawrence   65–7, 68–9, 87,
   93–4 (n17)
Stoppard, Tom   138
Stow, John   23, 31
Stubbes, Philip   13, 18, 32
Stubbs, Imogen   108, 129–30

Styan, J. L.   126
subjectivity, feminine   8
Survey of London, A (Stow)   23
Swetnam, Joseph   15

tavern, world: and lawlessness   37,
   40
Tearsheet, Doll, *Henry IV, Part 1*
   36, 38–9
Tell-Trothes New-Yeares Gift   82
text, embodying   104–8
textile industry   27–8
theatre: directors and female roles
   106; gestic   126; hierarchies
   105; players and scholars
   102–3; and theatricality   107,
   130–9
theatrical practice: and critical
   discourse   102–3; Shakespeare
   126
theatricality: and theatre   107;
   witches in *Macbeth*   1, 130–9
Totem and Taboo (Freud)   62–3
tradition   113
tragic ending: genre and ideology
   86–8
Traub, Valerie   89–90 (n10), 92
   (n11)
Troilus and Cressida   102, 104,
   119–21
Trussler, Simon   129
Two Noble Kinsmen, The   122–5,
   129
Tybalt, *Romeo and Juliet*   76–7

Ulysses, *Troilus and Cressida*   102,
   104
Utile Dulce: Or Trueths Libertie
   (Erasmus)   16–17

venereal disease   31

Vincentio, Duke of Vienna 41,
42–3, 45
victimization 31, 128
virtue 15, 18–19

wage economy 26, 27
Wallerstein, Immanuel 96 (n25)
Weimann, Robert 110, 111, 143
(n12)
Weyward Sisters: carnivalesque
138–9; by female players 136;
by male players 135–6;
masquing 134–5; name 132;
platea 132; in production
141–2; theatricality 1, 130–9;
witch costumes 140–1; *see also*
Macbeth
Whetstone, George 82
White, Edmund 5
whores: and wives 14, 18, 46–7
Williams, David 128

Williams, Raymond 110, 113,
120, 121
witches: appearance (in *Macbeth*)
133–4; English 69–70;
liminality 131; players
135–6; theatricality 1, 130–9
wives: bond with husband 67; and
whores 14, 18, 46–7
women: employment opportunities
26, 27–8; identity 10–11;
immorality 15; passivity 16;
in rebellion 8–9; Renaissance
ideal 15; *see also* female sexuality
Women in the Middle Ages and the
Renaissance 9
Worthen, William 127
Wright, George 123, 124
Wrightson, Keith 66–7

Zaretsky, Eli 62, 65